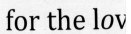 for the lov

C000246970

for the love not the glory

DAVE WORTON

LED ASTRAY

Thanks to Becky and Molly Worton; Matt Reeder, Rhys Howell, Finola Fitzpatrick and everyone at the *Harrogate Advertiser*; Matt Kirkham for going above the call of duty to let me use his photographs free of charge; Jordan Ford for help with detail in a few of the columns and for organising away travel; Mike Whorley, Jack Wilkinson, Rich Hawley and Steve Riding for other photographs; and, last but not least, Martin Callaghan for kind words, encouragement and proof-reading: *'Don't refer to Salford as Manchester'* and *'What is a three man central back four?'*

All uncredited photographs were taken by the author. Yes, I know I'm no Matt Kirkham, but I think they make a nice contrast to his professional ones.

Front cover photo: Mill Farm, AFC Fylde, February 2020.
Back cover photo: Holker Street, Barrow, August 2019.

for the love not the glory

Introduction

It's funny the way life can take you in unexpected directions.

Four and a half years ago, I attended a Harrogate Town match with my daughter, Molly, expecting it to be a one off. It wasn't, and we fell in love with a football club.

I'd been a lifelong Wolverhampton Wanderers' fan up to that point, even founding and editing the fanzine *'A Load Of Bull'* way back in the late eighties/early nineties. Molly wasn't even into football until that fateful day.

After two and a bit seasons addictively following Town in the National League North, the club achieved promotion to the National League for the first time in its history. It inspired me to start writing again, and I decided to catalogue the journey to promotion as witnessed by my daughter and I.

I figured I'd send the article to *'When Saturday Comes'* and other football publications in the hope of getting it printed. And, I reasoned to myself that, if nobody wanted it, it would be a piece of writing that I would leave with my daughter as a memory of our adventures together.

I duly sent it to *'When Saturday Comes'* and received a rejection email from Andy Lyons of said publication within three and a half hours. My article was too long and they'd published a Harrogate Town article only recently. It was and they had, albeit a slightly detached piece coming nowhere near to touching on the passion of this club. At least he was kind enough to let me down gently and, although he couldn't possibly know it at the time, he did me a favour in the long run.

A little deflated and unsure what to do next, I decided to send it to the *Harrogate Advertiser*, not expecting to hear back. Within an hour, Matt Reeder, the content editor, had replied to me saying he loved it, asking if they could reproduce it in next week's paper. It was too long, of course, so it would need editing down... I was thrilled. Of course they could. And that was that. Or so I thought.

On the eve of the first National League season, Matt got in touch with me again. Would I like to write a weekly column for the *Advertiser*?

He went on to explain, *'We want to avoid the usual player column and see if we can do something a little different. My editor is very keen as she loved your end-of-season piece and really likes the idea that you go along with your daughter each week. All we would be looking for is about 300-350 words every week to run in the Harrogate Advertiser sports pages. Not so much about the football itself, but about the fan side of things, the stories from the terraces, the funny things you see or the things that fans are unhappy about.'*

What was not to like?

'Sadly we do not have any budget for payment... but you will have the honour of writing for the Advertiser!'

Ah...

It didn't need much thought, though, and I tentatively submitted my first column, worried that it wouldn't be what they were looking for. I remember talking to Matt on the phone, saying I was conscious of the fact that I wasn't writing just for football fanzine reading fans anymore, I was writing for anyone who picked the newspaper up, whether they were into football or not, and it was important to try and appeal to everyone. I wasn't sure whether I was achieving that. He replied that it was the eternal dilemma of all good writers.

Of course, those 300-350 words soon grew into 700 words and then into 1,300, as the column blossomed into a full page of the newspaper and my confidence grew.

From early on, I'd been sending my columns to a friend of mine at work. He'd edited *'Slag!'* fanzine (a Wakefield must-read back in the previous century), written for various football publications and was a semi-regular on the *'When Saturday Comes'* letters pages. One day he commented, *'I really enjoy reading these. I'm struck by the interaction between yourself and your daughter,'* and, remembering the *Advertiser* editor's earlier comments, I determined to make that a feature of the columns whenever I possibly could.

Of course I wanted to deal with the playing side of things, but I also wanted to tell a story, to make people laugh, to laugh at myself, to appeal to the person who wasn't into football or Harrogate Town at all, or the person who only came to the odd match. After all, it's not that I went to every match myself; sometimes life just got in the way. I wanted to convey the sheer sense of excitement that comes with following a small football team with my daughter and others, whether it be from inside the ground, on a coach or sitting in a car park listening to the radio. I wanted it to strike a chord with everybody, not just the regulars that go home and away every week.

It just so transpired that Town happened to be in the form of their lives. I guess you could say I was in the right place at the right time.

So the *Advertiser* got something *'a little different'*, although I'm not quite sure it's what they were expecting when we set out, as I recalled tales of inadvertent shoplifting and sickness on the Stray, together with little snippets of conversations, even managing to get the word *'bum'* into one headline. Surely some sort of first for the *Advertiser*.

To their credit, they've supported everything I've written. After all, these tales are there to draw the reader into a column stained through, like the writing in a stick of rock, with a love of Harrogate Town and everybody involved in it. Yes, even the column on my boyhood love of Gornal Athletic and visiting my grandad.

I never saw much feedback for what I was writing, apart from staff at the *Advertiser* and a few fans passing on words of encouragement. Then, on a coach trip to Fylde, a fellow fan and supermarket boss told me my column was the first thing three of his employees turned to every week as soon as the paper arrived in store. When he had enquired why, the response was along the lines of, *'Have you read it? It's the funniest thing in the paper.'* None of them were particularly into football. That well and truly made my week.

I'd no intention of writing this book when I started out, but events overtook me. Incredibly, Town achieved promotion to the Football League in a season like no other. A season scarred by a global pandemic.

I did my best to keep writing throughout this time and I think the results accurately mirror the uncertainties, fears and eventual boredom of lockdown, from the initial feeling of a bizarre kind of novelty to there being nothing much left to write about for a while, as coronavirus raged and society closed down.

Deciding to paste all my articles into one document during lockdown, I realised I'd easily accumulated enough for a book.

My aforementioned work friend had been encouraging me to publish my columns for a while, so I thought, *'why not?'*

Although the *Advertiser* did their very best to print what I wrote unedited most weeks, space constraints occasionally came into play as my submissions grew in length. If the newspaper columns are to be regarded as a serious of 7 inch singles, this book recalls some of them in 12 inch extended remix format.

Like the team, some weeks are better than others, but the writing is always honest. I hope you enjoy the helter-shelter ride through four years of growth and wide-eyed excitement both on and off the pitch. Please forgive my occasional contradictions, the odd 'preachy' bit, wrong prediction whilst in lockdown and all. It's funny, but I always tried to steer away from speculation, living totally for the moment, week to week, until the mind-numbing experience of lockdown left us all with nothing else.

The results of my endeavours are here before you and tell a story like no other in Town's history.

Of course we're far from out of the woods pandemic-wise and, with infections again rising steeply going into winter, and plans to return fans to the grounds currently on indefinite hold, the first Football League season in Town's history is going to be a thrilling yet strange and difficult one in many ways.

At times, I felt an overarching feeling of sadness, alongside the joy of remembrance, when compiling the pictures for the centre pages of this book. It was a sadness for that which we've currently lost; a sense of joy, community and togetherness inside a football ground. We should never forget, though, that many people have lost, and stand to lose, much more than that.

As we learn to live with coronavirus, and social distancing measures become the norm, it's shaping up to be another huge journey into the unknown. All I can do is continue to take each week as it comes.

Hopefully the *Advertiser* will want me to keep writing about it.

Dave Worton
Harrogate, October 2020

Chapter One
I started something
I couldn't finish

Life in the National League North
2016/18

A sense of belonging

Article originally edited down and published on Thursday 31st May 2018 in a two page spread under the title *'Part of the Harrogate family – how Town stole our hearts.'*

I can't remember the exact reason now. Maybe I was avoiding a mind-numbing trip to Ikea but, whatever the circumstances, I can't specifically recall what motivated me that particular weekend, just over two years ago, to visit Harrogate Town's Wetherby Road ground for the first time in a good while.

Being a lifelong Wolverhampton Wanderers follower, having moved from the Midlands to Leeds in the early eighties, I'd had a somewhat minor relationship with Harrogate and local non-league football in general. I've fond, but faint, memories of getting the train from Burley Park to watch Town on Tuesday nights in the late 1980's, when Wolves weren't playing of course, and then attending occasional matches over the next decade. I moved within a chant's reach of Wetherby Road in 2004, but rarely ventured into the ground unless Town were in the First Round of the FA Cup or if the gates happened to be open when I sauntered past, fifteen minutes from the end of the game.

I'll let you into a little secret; I wasn't being straight with you. I can remember why I went to watch Town that particular Saturday just over two years ago. It was because FC United of Manchester were the visitors and I thought it would be interesting to watch a match in front of a big boisterous travelling crowd.

I got what I expected alright, but not quite in the way I'd expected. True, FC United bought a large, brash following, swelling the crowd into four figures, but they were thrashed 5-0 by a buoyant Town side playing great football and, get this, roared on by their own vociferous support.

Things had changed. Gone were the 200 or so stoic regulars huddled under the Wetherby Road stand on a rainy Tuesday night, except they were still there of course, but now supplemented by a noisy Kop in the end behind the goal and a vibrant family-friendly atmosphere. Even the shirts were brighter than I remembered.

I was immediately hooked, as was my eleven year old daughter. The conversation pre-match had gone something like this:

'Do you want to go to the football match?'

'No, not really, dad, it'll be boring.'

'Well I'm going anyway, see you later...'

'OK, I suppose I'll come as I've nothing better to do.'

Now she was leaving the ground with a scarf saying *'Can we come to the next match? When is it? How does the new offside rule work?'* The answers were *'Yes,'* *'Next week,'* and *'Nobody's got the foggiest, let alone the officials.'*

My footballing mojo was well and truly back, having been previously beaten into submission by a Chinese corporation owned professional club; constantly changing managers in a fit of pique and deluded sense of entitlement. I'm talking Wolves, but I could be talking Leeds and any number of others.

We attended until the disappointment of the end of season Play-Off Semi-Final defeat to Fylde and then became fully fledged Yellow/Black Army conscripts in the 2016/17 season.

She cottoned on fairly quickly, did my daughter. Hating Brendan Daniels, our sporadically brilliant attacking winger, for signing for the *'enemy'* Fylde and looking forward to the distant March date when she could tell him how she felt at Wetherby Road. She also picked up pretty quickly on Jack Emmett, our own local lad made good, announcing him as her favourite player a whole season before I realised he was my favourite player too, once Simon Weaver moved him from the wing into centre-attacking midfield.

We were present at The Shay to see our Jack hammer in the only goal of the game from distance in our first full season and then watched Halifax fans boo fan hero Lloyd Kerry for 'time-wasting' when he went down late on with an injury, before getting up and walking slowly off the pitch. It turned out that he only had a fractured eye socket.

One highlight from that season was hanging on to defeat Bradford Park Avenue 1-0 at home, despite only having nine men left on the pitch. Our goal machine, Simon Ainge, having been sent off for a seemingly innocuous foul in front of the corner flag by a card-happy referee. I work with someone who used to play for Bradford Park Avenue, and have it on good authority that the offending Bradford defender felt a touch from Ainge before collapsing like he'd been shot from behind, all with a melodramatic yelp added in for good effect. To rub salt into Bradford's wounds, our keeper Peter Crook saved a penalty. And the rebound.

We were there as the aforementioned central-defender turned emergency-centre-forward-in-an-injury-crisis Ainge banged (well mostly headed) in goal after goal, becoming the second highest scorer in the country behind Harry Kane. It was an even more impressive stat when you realise he played the first four months of the season in central defence. There was one spell in the season when every Joe Leesley cross seemed to unerringly find his head like a guided missile.

The season ended in anti-climax as Town slipped out of the play-off positions but it had still been a season of improvement off the pitch, with the average crowd nudging towards 1,000 and a vast repertoire of songs taking shape for every player.

The real change came the following season, with the club going professional for the first time in their history. Everything suddenly seemed to step up a notch, both on and off the pitch. The promise of a full time contract allowed Town to attract great players such as Josh Falkingham and George Thomson from Darlington and FC United, to supplement the young, hungry nucleus of an already strong squad.

Meanwhile our songsmiths in the crowd kept pace admirably, composing gems such as *'He's only four foot two but he's better than you'* (Josh Falkingham) and *'There's a star man playing on the right, his name is Georgie Thomson and his feet are dynamite'* (guess who). Warren Burrell, our talisman, even had a banner dedicated to him. I just wish someone would work out a better song for Jack Emmett.

My favourite chant of the season, however, was reserved for the visit of Penistone Church in the Second Qualifying Round of the FA Cup. The Church bought around a hundred for their big day out and their fans elected to stand in the Kop next to the Town fans. The chant went up from the home fans, *'Shall we sing a song for you?'* On garnering no response, there was a long pause before one Town wag started up with *'All Things Bright and Beautiful...'* Church lost, but it was fantastic to see the enthusiasm and commitment of their supporters and players. You just don't get this kind of entertainment in the money-grabbing, penalty-diving Premier League.

The players played some spellbinding football at times, notching a hundred league goals in the process and only failing to score twice. *'It was just like watching Brazil,'* remarked one fan I met on his way back from Stockport early in the season. This bizarrely was the only time Town didn't win in the first seven matches.

Other highlights included a trip to Southport on a filthy Tuesday night. Free beer, pizza and chips on the coach (don't expect this every time prospective away trippers) preceded a 4-1 victory in the pouring rain during which the 30+ strong away following didn't stop singing for virtually the whole ninety minutes. We raced into a 4-0 half-time lead at home to Alfreton, taking us back to the top of the league, and then had to suffer the jitters as our opponents, Brendan Daniels and all, came a world class James Belshaw save away from squaring at 4-4. A hapless FC United were duly dispatched again, 6-0 this time.

Then there was York City. Twice.

Who would have believed that little old Harrogate Town would become North Yorkshire's top team, doing the double over their larger neighbours in the process. Both matches remain etched in the memory. An unsegregated 2,800 at Wetherby Road in September and a 2-0 win, summed up perfectly by the Harrogate-based York fan on Facebook who moaned that he'd supported City all his life and had proudly taken his young son along to watch them for the first time... and now his son had repaid him by wanting to support Harrogate Town. Worse still, he wanted a Town shirt. Oh how I felt for his dad. Being saddled with York City, that is.

The match at Bootham Crescent was even better. Town took an unprecedented 515 supporters and Jake Wright became a new folk hero.

Of course, there were downs as well. In March, whilst celebrating a routine home win to Gainsborough with the players, fake news came through that Kidderminster had hung on to defeat rivals Salford 4-3. We were back at the top on goal difference and celebrated with the manager and players in front of the Kop. Then the tannoy crackled back into action: *'The news from Kidderminster is that Salford have pulled it back to 4-4.'* Our bubble was well and truly burst.

Town frustratingly suffered only their second home defeat of the season in the following game, 2-1 to a cynical time wasting Spennymoor team, handing the advantage back to Salford in the process. I must, however, commend the victorious North East players on taking the time to remind the Kop of how many goals they'd scored via considerate use of hand signals.

We just lost out to Salford for the title, but gave them a run for their money, clawing back an eleven point deficit at one point. Common wisdom will tell you we finished second because we lost twice to Salford in the course of the season. Just one win for us would have seen Town promoted. But I maintain it was Salford's 'dirty tricks' department, coming in for our goal and assist machine Leesley in December and turning his head just long enough to contribute to us dropping five points against FC United and Kidderminster. They've now departed company with their managers on achieving promotion. Enough said.

All of this excitement has led to a steady increase in crowds to a season's average of over four figures. No one knows this more acutely than my daughter and I, as we've been playing 'Predict The Crowd' since we started attending, and now we can no longer cheat by counting heads during an extended injury break. I once got the crowd figure spot on during an early game and my daughter must have thought I had psychic powers of perception. She now knows it was just a fluke.

The crowd hit 1,170 for the end of season match against Curzon Ashton when Town had already secured second place and chose to rest a few players. Four years ago it may have attracted 300 odd. But there were no Curzon hordes to swell the crowd here, it was almost entirely Town fans, and maybe a few disaffected Leeds fans. The attendance was rewarded with a five goal haul for Dom Knowles to take us to the aforementioned ton, two of them in added-on time. I'd seen Steve Bull clatter in the majority of his 306 goals in thirteen years at Wolves, but I'd never seen him do this. Wolves may have emerged from the chaos of the last few years and run away with The Championship, and I'd enjoyed watching from afar, but Town had stolen my heart.

In the Play-Off Semi-Final, Town completely over-ran visitors Chorley with slick, incisive passing movements and waves of attacks for the first half an hour, but the visitors' goal led a charmed life. When Chorley scored from their first chance on goal, heads dropped and nerves set into the crowd.

Cue the unusual sight of the Managing Director walking along the Wetherby Road Stand waving his arms and shouting at the crowd to turn the volume back up. Then Town were awarded a penalty. Chorley fans ran forward and shook the net, it seemed to take an eternity for things to calm down, and when Knowles eventually despatched it, I couldn't believe it had gone in. I was just too tense to celebrate. Ten men Chorley then basically shut up shop and we were heading into extra time when a speculative shot fell to Knowles in the fourth minute of injury time, for him to make it 2-1. I was sure he was offside. He had to be offside. I just stared at the linesman, awaiting the inevitable flag. It never came. The crowd went crazy like I'd never seen at Town before. In retrospect, I could have saved myself all that worry if I'd realised it was always meant to be. The Chorley manager had been cursed by the National League North Manager of the Month award prior to kick off.

A capacity 3,000 crammed into Wetherby Road for the Play-Off Final, general sale tickets disappearing within twenty four hours. Two more goals from Knowles and one from the National League North Player of the Season, Leesley, only told half the story. Town had two players stretchered off before half-time and, for all the talk of the visitors' mean defence, it was Town who defended like their lives depended on it when they had to.

It turned out to be Brackley who couldn't live with our pace and attacking desire, as evidenced by the third goal. As soon as Kerry nicked the ball in deep midfield, Ryan Fallowfield, our effervescent young full back raced down the right wing, hand aloft in the air. The ball to him was decent if slightly over hit, but Ryan wasn't letting it go out as he burst every sinew to reach it, before teeing up an incoming Leesley right in front of us in the Kop end.

We'd done it, we'd reached the top tier of non-league football: a whole tier above York City. It was two amazing firsts for little old Town.

My thoughts on the 3G pitch? First season it was installed, I wasn't sure I'd warm to it, but I did, straight away. I occasionally miss a good old muddy goalmouth scramble, although our trip to rainy Salford fulfilled that craving this year. The pitch allows Town to get the ball down and play football the way it's meant to be played, whilst bringing both money and the local community into the club seven days a week, even when it's chucking it down with rain. Most of Harrogate is built on clay and the artificial pitch became a necessity if Town were to ever progress. You only have to witness the two months of home postponements for relegated Harrogate Railway this year, or the fixture pile-up which caused Spennymoor to resort to playing two games a week on Town's 3G surface, to realise that, with our old waterlogged pitch, we'd have had as much chance of promotion as York, once we'd burned ourselves out catching up eight games in three weeks. Now all we need is for the Football League to take their collective heads out of the sand with regards to policy on this.

The thing I love most though about Town is the togetherness of the club and supporters and the air of continuity, having had the same manager for seven years. *'That's because while his dad's the owner, he'll never go anywhere,'* said the few doubters when we lost out to Salford for top spot. Fair point, but that's not a negative in my book. Simon Weaver has the top job on his own merits and, as far as

I'm concerned, as long as he wants it. Irving Weaver came in after his son, not the other way around, and I, for one, am glad he did. The club is well run and looking towards steady progression and consolidation both on and off the pitch with the move to full time football and plans to develop the ground into a 5,000 capacity stadium. Trouble is, all this talk of steady, gradual progression may go out of the window if this team keeps performing the way it has done this season.

Bring it on, I say. We've got season tickets.

Chapter Two
Into the unknown

A first season in the National League
2018/19

Here comes the weekend, I get to see the Town

Sutton United (H) D 2-2. Goals: Muldoon, Langmead. Crowd: 1,378. Article originally published in a severely edited down past-tense version on Thursday 9th August 2018 under the title *'Town fan's perspective of the Sutton United game.'*

Excitement, tinged with apprehension. I think that sums up my feelings approaching the big kick-off against Sutton United. I'm still pinching myself that it's actually for real, that Town are one (admittedly huge) step away from the Football League. Today we find out just how good we are, against a team that finished third in the National League last season.

Molly and I arrive early, keen to soak up the atmosphere and catch the £5 kit bargains on the club shop sale rail. My daughter lucks in on a home shirt with no advertising on the front, just like in the old days. The other big news of the day is that chips are back on the menu at the snack bars.

We take up our first half position in the Wetherby Road Stand next to an elderly gent who proceeds to ask me who Town's best players are. Of course, I take him through the entire team, before asking him if this is his first match. *'No,'* he replies, *'I'm a Sutton fan.'*

As Town tear into the visitors in the first thirty minutes, he then proceeds to let out a series of 'oohs' and 'ahs,' simultaneously grabbing my arm every time Town go close. He just can't believe the football we're playing, even their goalkeeper's reduced to wasting time twenty minutes in. Then, when Sutton win a free kick in a dangerous area, I tell him this is our occasional Achilles' heel.

Oh me and my big mouth.

Despite looking down and out of it either side of half-time against a strong, physical side, Town claw their way back into the game. The equaliser brings scenes of delirium in the Kop end and there's even a tentative, tongue-in-cheek chant of *'We're on our way to the Football League.'* At 2-1 the chant is tempered to *'Staying Up.'* We won't dare to dream just yet.

Can we hold on? It looks like we might, but visiting hands shoot up into the air at the other end and the referee points to the spot. You can hear a pin drop in the Town end. Disappointment ensues, but not for long, as we'd have taken this at half-time. It's early days, but we've made one of last season's best look ordinary at times and I think the elderly gent will be heading back down south relieved with the point.

The chips weren't bad either.

I can't stand up for falling down

Hartlepool United (A) D 2-2. Goals: Knowles, Howe. Crowd: 3,623. Bromley (A) D 1-1. Goal: Knowles. Crowd: 1,081. Barnet (H) W 2-0. Goals: Emmett, Kitching. Crowd: 1,381. Article originally published on Thursday 16th August 2018 under the title *'Decision to segregate fans is a mystery to me, but what a great start'*

One of the great joys of supporting Harrogate Town at Wetherby Road is the ability to watch the match with my daughter from whichever vantage⁻ point we choose, unhindered by needless fencing. Town fans are a vocal but friendly lot, so segregation is the exception rather than the rule, and the club should be commended for that.

Unfortunately, one of the drawbacks of Town's exciting upward journey is the encountering of more segregation the higher we climb. The opening two away matches at Hartlepool and Bromley were such affairs, although quite why Bromley, with a support base similar to Town, should choose to segregate sixty away fans is a total mystery.

Segregation at Hartlepool was understandable, given their League history and large following, however the home welcome to the large Town following was cordial, with supporters mixing happily in the pubs beforehand. A large proportion of Town fans chose to stand to cheer the team on in the all-seated away end. Somewhat bizarrely, just before half-time, a lone steward was seen trying to encourage a solitary fan in a completely empty section of seats to sit down *'for safety reasons'*. He ultimately failed in his mission and gave up.

Cue the first Town equaliser and one of our own fans accidentally flinging himself down four rows of seats in his over-excitement, busting his nose in the process and having to receive first aid. Don't worry, dear reader, Jordan's fine, if a little embarrassed. While I wholeheartedly support him in making the case for safe standing, I made a mental note not to stand next to him in the seats in future and exited at the end past a lone steward muttering *'Told you so.'*

So, one win and three draws in our opening four matches, with goalkeeper James Belshaw performing absolute miracles in both the Bromley and Barnet matches. We're not going to roll teams over like last season and there will be spells when we have to defend for our lives, but we're more than capable of taking the game to the opposition. This is a tough league, and to say I'm happy so far would be an understatement.

On my radio

Aldershot Town (A) W 2-0. Goals: Knowles, Thomson. Crowd: 1,774.
Article originally published on Thursday 23rd August 2018 under
the title *'Nirvana found in Halifax car park as fine start continues.'*

When I was approached by the *Advertiser* to consider
writing this column, I felt it only fair to warn the Editor that
although I had a home season ticket, I wouldn't be attending
every away match, unlike some of our more dedicated
supporters. He assured me that was fine as they didn't expect
me to. It's just as well, because this week I was reduced to
driving around Halifax trying to find a stable Radio York
signal in order to follow the match at Aldershot. I achieved
nirvana in the car park of a well-known budget superstore in
the shadow of the Shay Stadium, but not before missing the
first goal due to a loss of reception as I passed the train
station. *'Knowles is through, Town must score here ... crackle,
hiss, pop...'*

Aargh!

Halifax were at home across the road and the Premier
League was on crisp, clear Radio 5, but I wasn't visiting either
of those places if there was a chance of tuning into a distant
Barry Parker.

All's well that ends well. I caught the second goal and
Barry informed us that the Aldershot commentators were
remarking how Town had no need for a goalkeeper; such was
the bluntness of the home attack against the Town defence.
What a difference a week makes!

Reverting to more modern technology, I texted my daughter, who was down the road at grandma's, to the tune of *'2-0 Town.'* Back came the one word reply *'Yay!!'*

Just a mobile phone and an internet connection can get you up-to-the-minute news on Twitter, but there's still something indescribably exciting about listening to a crackly radio commentary in the back end of nowhere, especially when you finally tune into National BBC Radio 5 at 5pm for Sports Report and hear *'Aldershot Town 0'* ... (slightly rising voice) *'Harrogate Town 2'.*

Another great result, our first away victory in the National League and the team is showing every sign of growing quickly into this level. To quote a supporter on Facebook, *'I was almost looking forward to a nice quiet mid-table season, you know, get the blood pressure down, and the lads are doing this to me.'* I couldn't have put it better myself.

Giant killers

Solihull Moors (H) W 3-1. Goals: Kitching, Thomson, Howe. Crowd: 1,180. AFC Fylde (A) D 0-0. Crowd: 1,709. Article originally published on Thursday 30th August 2018 under the title *'We're exceeding expectations but early injuries are a concern.'*

With early season pace setters Wrexham losing a couple of hours earlier, a win at second placed AFC Fylde in front of the live BT Sport Cameras would have taken Town to the top of the National League.

I'll pause, and let that opening sentence sink in for a moment, because in spite of my optimism for the new season in a piece I wrote following promotion, and the belief that Simon Weaver has assembled a team more than capable of holding its own in this league, it's truly a sentence I never saw coming.

Of course, we didn't win at Fylde and didn't serve up a goal feast in front of the cameras, but a goalless draw against a team that had won their previous three home matches, contains the goal machine Danny Rowe and was seeking to go top also, was a brilliant result. Town certainly won off the pitch though, with the travelling fans singing for virtually the entire ninety minutes, picking up compliments from the BT pundits and Fylde fans along the way.

Couple this with the hard-earned home victory two days before against a team seemingly composed of towering giants from the Midlands, and it's turned out to be rather a good week, especially as two of our three goals in that match were the result of headers from corners.

It's here, however, that I seek to strike a slight note of caution. There's concern amongst fans that our squad is a little thin on the ground to cope with the stresses of a more physically demanding league. Last season, we were lucky with injuries, and were able to field a strong, settled team consistently. This season, early injuries to three of our key players, midfielders Falkingham, Emmett and full back Fallowfield, are already beginning to test our small squad to its limits. Although we have cover on the bench, and two or three players who can be employed in different positions, we can't afford to pick up many more knocks.

Still, the club has used the loan market to good advantage in recent times and I remain hopeful that, if required, a couple of good quality additions can be found, especially in light of our strong start.

We are the road crew.
No sleep 'til Gateshead

Eastleigh (H) W 4-0. Goals: Muldoon 2, Beck 2. Crowd: 1,158.
Gateshead (A) W 3-2. Goals: Knowles (pen), Muldoon, Williams.
Crowd: 846. Article originally published on Thursday 6th September
2018 under the title *Gateshead on a Tuesday night – the best trip I've
ever been on.*

'Weaver had a dream, to reach the National League, he tried for years and now his dream has come true. Don't wanna go home, don't wanna go home, this is the best trip I've ever been on.'

It's not quite how I'd choose to describe a trip to Gateshead on a Tuesday night, but I'm on a noisy Supporters' Club coach sat near to a fan resplendent in a dayglo yellow suit, tie and hat, nicely complimented with a black shirt. It turns out Craig was born in Gateshead before coming to Harrogate, but I'm not sure he has to go to such lengths to prove he's a Town fan now!

I'm bleary-eyed and tired after a long day at work into the bargain. And that's before the match has even started. Sleep is out of the question, though, as we disembark near the ground and head into *'The Schooner'*, a local Motorhead-themed pub that bills itself as *'the second best bar in Gateshead.'* It's also rumoured to be haunted.

The Gateshead Stadium is modern, all-seated and totally characterless with a running track separating us from the pitch. It's hard to get any sort of atmosphere going in a place such as this, but we try our best.

To their credit, a decent home team try to play the game the right way and, after going 1-0 up, we ride our luck at times. At 2-2, with ten minutes to go, the players look dead on their legs. But the spirit of this squad is incredible.

Then, much-needed substitute Williams scuffs a shot, a few minutes after coming on, and it crawls past a static keeper for his first Harrogate goal. Unbelievably, with Wrexham drawing, little old Town go top!!

All that's left is a happy but stunned coach journey home and an alarm call at six 'o' clock for a long day of tiresome meetings. But no matter, as I'll be sat there happily dreaming of Saturday to come and wondering whether a yellow suit would help to liven the proceedings up.

Oh, and I take it back. This is the best trip that I've ever been on.

A different kind
of tension

Havant & Waterlooville (H) W 3-2. Goals: Howe, Knowles, Muldoon. Crowd: 1,709. Article originally published on Thursday 13th September 2018 under the title *'Enjoying every single minute of marvellous adventure.'*

The season so far has been a marvellous adventure into unchartered waters, and I've enjoyed nearly every minute of it. This weekend, however, felt different and the nerves hit me early on the Saturday morning. Reaching the dizzy heights of league leaders had raised the stakes and, although my head tells me the play-offs would be a major achievement, my stomach desperately wanted the team to win and stay top.

The Havant And Waterlooville game also raised the stakes in the attendance department, with just over 1,700 attending, and you could sense the increase in atmosphere. Maybe some of the new fans attending due to the international break will get the same buzz of excitement my daughter and I got three years ago, and decide to come back.

The pressure of being leaders appeared to hit the players as well, as we started slowly, struggling to retain possession and finding ourselves one down inside five minutes. What an equaliser though! After great pressure from Town, a superb Leesley cross setting up a bullet header from Howe. Standing in the Kop, I was struck by how loud the roar around the ground was.

Without Falkingham and Emmett pulling the strings, we play a slightly different way, but boy have Kerry and Agnew stepped in. Three wins out of three since they came into the team says it all. Yes, we were pinned back at times, and the last twenty minutes were unbearably tense, but what excitement! The team were unplayable for the decisive spell just after half-time and the back line defended for dear life after that.

The man in black had the worst game I've seen since the referee that sent two Town players off against Bradford Park Avenue two seasons ago. I lost count of the times he awarded free kicks to the visitors for seemingly non-existent fouls. Kerry was booked for a 'second' offence, when his first talking to was for a clean interception in midfield with opponent left untouched. We tried to tell him in no uncertain terms, but he just got worse. The second goal for the visitors resulted from a free kick awarded in similar mysterious circumstances.

My daughter has a theory that the more the crowd gets upset with an official, the more obstinate he becomes. She could well be right.

I'm just a jealous guy, as wife is handed trophy for safe-keeping

Maidstone United (A) W 2-0. Goals: Howe, Muldoon. Crowd: 2,222.
Article originally published on Thursday 20th September 2018
under the title *'Insanely jealous of wife's picture with National League
trophy'*

Today my wife returned from work with a photograph of herself holding the National League North trophy. To say I was completely shocked is an understatement, as she hates football. The only time I've ever been with her to a match, she spent the whole time counting the crowd out of sheer boredom, whilst a controversial four goal thriller ensued on the pitch in front of us. So how on earth did she manage to get her hands on such a coveted item?

Well, it turns out Town representatives were at neighbouring Willow Tree School talking to the children and showing them the trophy. On seeing our new Community Development Manager snowed under with a mountain of stuff, she offered to help him carry something and he handed her the trophy. She asked for a photo with it as her husband and daughter are huge fans and, of course, I'm insanely jealous.

The professional way in which Town saw out the second half at MUFC (we can but dream) whilst sitting on a two goal lead, bodes well for the season ahead. We handled a potential banana skin against a Maidstone team seeking to impress their new manager very well. With injured players coming back to fitness, the entire squad will have a vital part to play in the next few weeks.

Town fans spoke very highly of the welcome from the Kent club, with the stewards even allowing the younger travelling fans on to the 3G pitch at the end to celebrate with the players. Viewing the pictures on Twitter, the joyful faces are a sight to behold, and that's just the players.

Eleven games in is normally a good benchmark to assess progress, but I think a better indication will be after the two massive home games against third and second placed Leyton Orient and Wrexham this week. A few years ago, these would have been huge FA Cup ties, now we're playing as equals. Orient arrive on the crest of an undefeated eleven game run also and the game is unsegregated, so Town fans are aiming to claim the Kop early on Saturday to roar the team on. My daughter is gutted at having to miss it, so I'm going to have to shout twice as loud.

Shoplifters of the world unite, as the Orient express steams into Town

Leyton Orient (H) L 0-3. Crowd: 2,584. Wrexham (H) D 0-0. Crowd: 2,387. Article originally published on Thursday 27th September 2018 under the title *'Preoccupation with Town has turned me into a criminal.'*

I wish to confess to a crime, and it's all Harrogate Town's fault.

Whilst tucking into a French stick for lunch last weekend with my family, my daughter enquired innocently as to how much it had cost. It was only then I realised with horror that I hadn't actually paid for it. I'd walked clean out of Marks and Spencers, past the checkouts and store detective, brandishing the offending article whilst daydreaming about the upcoming Leyton Orient match.

This is what Town are doing to me.

On realising I'd absent-mindedly stolen the bread we were eating, my wife wasn't at all surprised, but my daughter was a little concerned.

'Will you be arrested?' she worriedly enquired.

'Yes, probably,' I said ...'but you'll go down with me for handling stolen goods.'*

'I won't, will I?'

We finished the meal as fugitives and, before you, dear reader, report me for shoplifting, I then crawled back to the shop with a sheepish look and 85p in a sweaty palm, to be met by a bemused and amused shop assistant.

Luckily, I escaped a prison sentence and made it to the Orient match. Did I say, luckily? Maybe 3-0 was a bit harsh, but Town were beaten for the first time this season by a clinical, experienced and well-organised visiting team. Emotions among the fans were a little raw after the match, as we're not used to losing, but the realisation soon sunk in that we had been beaten by the better team on the day. Town weren't that far behind though and, with a bit of luck, could have had a goal or two themselves.

There's certainly something magical about playing under lights, and so the following Tuesday night crackled with atmosphere. Fat queues huddled on Wetherby Road prior to kick off and a large expectant crowd made themselves heard, including a sizeable following from North Wales.

The match was always tense, if a little cagey at times, and you got the impression that both teams would settle for a point after heavy defeats at the weekend. Town tore into Wrexham early on and should have been a goal up, but the visitors had a strong second half showing and we had Belshaw and a dogged defensive performance to thank yet again.

I was certainly happy with the point. As we learned last year with Salford, if you can't beat the teams around you, then don't lose to them.

Thirteen games in, we've played all of the top nine except Salford (and ourselves of course), we've yet to play four of the bottom five, and we sit third in the table. I'd have snapped your hand off for that in August.

Smells like team spirit

Boreham Wood (A) W 4-2. Goals: Thomson, Williams, o.g., Emmett. Crowd: 566. Article originally published on Thursday 4th October 2018 under the title *'Togetherness the key as Town make a return to winning ways.'*

Following testing matches against Orient and Wrexham, the big question was could Town get their season back on track against Boreham Wood?

Perhaps incredibly for a small commuter town flanked by the larger towns of Watford, St. Albans and the London Borough of Barnet, tiny Boreham Wood very nearly made it to the Football League last year, losing out only to Tranmere in the Play-Off Final at Wembley.

The town's major claim to fame though is being home to both Elstree Studios and the joyless Eastenders, and whilst it's fair to say that our visit provided drama galore, any comparisons to the long-running BBC soap end here, as this particular episode finished in a happy ending.

Unbeaten in six matches at home this season our Hertfordshire opponents were certainly no pushovers, and when they took an early lead, Town could have crumbled. That they didn't, going on to score four goals in the process, shows a team with fighting spirit and self-belief in abundance.

With two forwards, two attacking midfielders and a goalkeeper on the bench, Town were never going to settle for a draw and, following an unfortunate injury to Lloyd Kerry, the fit again Jack Emmett duly entered just before half-time to help change the course of the game (along with Joe Leesley's trademark crosses and Aaron Williams' backside).

It was like he'd never been away as he almost set up a goal immediately with a typical burst from midfield, and the home team struggled to cope thereafter with his pace and directness. If Boreham Wood had been watching Town in the last couple of weeks, they wouldn't have seen Emmett, so did he catch them unprepared?

Overall though, it was a superb team performance from a unified squad of players that continues to defy the odds. They're a team that deserves to be near the top of the league and, furthermore, one that's perfectly capable of staying there.

'Harrogate came here with a togetherness and a group of players who have gone up a level.' These are not my words, but those of Luke Garrard, the Boreham Wood manager. He may have just been talking about the team, but that *'togetherness'* at Town exists both on and off the pitch. Long may it continue.

Town Ladies upstage Liverpool and Manchester City

Ebbsfleet United (A) W 2-0. Goals: Howe, Williams. Crowd: 1,169.
Harrogate Town Ladies 4 Farsley Celtic Ladies 1. Crowd: 60(ish).
Article originally published on Thursday 11th October 2018 under
the title *'Entertained royally by Ladies' tidy brand of passing football.'*

With Town winning away down south for the second
Saturday running, and me not being able to go, I'm dependent
on Radio York again. Nonetheless, Barry Parker paints a
marvellous picture of a chaotic match played out in driving
wind and rain, as he and his co-commentator are forced to
seek shelter at the back of the stand with the home crowd in
order to save their computer equipment from drowning in a
ferocious downpour. The Premier League it certainly isn't.

Starved of action, and wishing to live up to the title of this
column, I saunter down to Wetherby Road on Sunday
afternoon to watch Harrogate Town Ladies in action against
Farsley Celtic, together with 60 or so other hardy souls.

Like the men, Town Ladies play a tidy brand of possession
football, pressing to win the ball and then playing out from
the back and through midfield. The left sided pair of Becky
Davies and Katie Rowlands remind me of Fallowfield and
Emmett, linking up and getting in behind, and the first two
goals of Sophie Tinson's latest hat-trick come via this route.

It's total one way traffic and 3-0 at half-time, spoiled only by the constant shouts of *'Man on!'* from two Farsley fans stood next to me. Someone really needs to tell them.

Strolling casually over to the queue-less refreshment kiosk, I spot *'Chip Butty 200p.'* Resisting the childish urge to go home and raid my daughter's penny jar to pay for it, I venture to the toilet first, safe in the knowledge that my chip butty awaits. On emerging, a queue of at least ten girls has appeared from absolutely nowhere in front of me. It turns out that they've all come with one of our near neighbours to watch their dance teacher play.

'What number is she?' I ask innocently.

'Number eleven,' comes the reply.

'Oh, she's really good, she's helped set up two of the goals,' I say.

'She plays for Farsley.'

We all agree, however, that it's really refreshing to see two teams of players just getting on with it. There's no histrionics when fouled, no haranguing the referee and no blame culture if someone makes a mistake.

In a quieter second half, Farsley pull one back and I contemplate leaving early as I have a date with a dog and Otley Chevin. I'm glad I don't.

With almost the last kick, Elisha James runs on to a loose ball and smashes a shot from the edge of the centre circle into the roof of the Farsley net past a startled keeper. It's an utterly fantastic goal. I exit the ground with a beaming smile, having being royally entertained for free.

Meanwhile, I hope you all enjoyed the Liverpool v Man City bore draw on TV.

Stubborn Dover refuse to roll over, but daughter's positivity wins the day

Dover Athletic (H) D 2-2. Goals: Williams, Langmead. Crowd: 1,865. Article originally published on Thursday 18th October 2018 under the title *'Supporters play their part as Dover forget to read the script.'*

'When you are going through hell, keep on going, never, never, never give up.'

That's all very well, but I'd venture that Winston Churchill didn't find his team deservedly 2-1 down to a stubborn Dover Athletic deep into injury time.

Having praised the players for their never-say-die spirit in previous columns, I find myself guilty of hypocrisy. If it wasn't enough that I'd totally given up on Town ever finding an equaliser, my daughter was also annoying me, harping on positively about how *'We're going to draw this, I can feel it.'*

Yet nothing was falling for us in the box and Dover had resorted to blatant time-wasting and injury-feigning to run the clock down. It was turning out to be *'one of those games.'*

Then, totally out of the blue, a great Langmead header levels it. I don't remember much else as delirium takes over in the Kop, apart from having to admit that my daughter was right, once it's all calmed down.

In the cold light of day, it was a lucky, but hard-earned, point against a second from bottom, under new management Dover team who clearly hadn't read the script. What made it a better result, though, was Salford and Orient dropping points in similar fashion.

On a different note, there's been a little concern this week amongst supporters that the usual singing section of the home crowd has seemed more subdued in recent times, despite the steady increase in attendances. A few theories have been put forward for this, but my own take on this is that the last three home matches have been more difficult ones for Town. The fighting spirit's been there, but the players have seen less of the ball and created less going forward, leading in turn to a little more anxiety in the stands.

However, it was nice that Simon Weaver recognised the positive contribution of the supporters towards that glorious late equaliser in his post-match interview, referring to us all as part of a team. Like my daughter, he's right. Both players and supporters raised their game and this will hopefully give us momentum going forward.

So let's start as we mean to continue, and sing the players into the FA Cup First Round proper on Saturday. Wouldn't it be nice to get there and draw Bradford City?* I bet they wouldn't dare send their reserves again.

*Bradford City severely underestimated Town pre-season and complacently sent a young team to play at Wetherby Road in a pre-season friendly, ending up on the end of an embarrassing seven goal thumping.

The Wrexham goal drought continues

Wrexham (H) D 0- 0 (FA Cup Fourth Qualifying Round). Crowd: 1,540. Wrexham (A) L 0-2 (FA Cup Fourth Qualifying Round Replay). Crowd: 2,550. Article originally published on Thursday 25th October 2018 under the title *'Disappointed to miss out on a trip to Weston-super-Mare.'*

Although I was tempted to make the arduous journey to North Wales on Tuesday night, work commitments put an abrupt end to any such thoughts.

Back in a previous life following Wolverhampton Wanderers, I was one of 400 lucky souls to draw a ticket for Torquay away in the Sherpa Van Trophy area final on a Tuesday night. I booked two days off work at the old Leeds Wholesale Markets on Pontefract Lane and headed down to the Midlands on the Monday evening to pick up a lift the following day. As bad luck would have it, the game was postponed for 24 hours.

This left me with a stark choice: stay in the Midlands and travel to the West Country on the Wednesday, or head off back up north to work. In reality, there was no competition. I chose the former and handed in my notice on returning to Yorkshire, probably before I was given the push.

So, feeling much more sensible and grown up, having lost that headstrong impulsiveness of youth, I'm sitting down to write this column at my kitchen table as Town and Wrexham are 235 minutes into a goalless stalemate.

Town may have played out another goalless draw against Wrexham in the FA Cup at Wetherby Road on Saturday, but the encounter was every bit as enthralling as the recent league match.

It was a great team effort, with the players rising to the noisy atmosphere generated by almost non-stop singing from the Town fans in the Wetherby Road stand. The full repertoire of Town songs was aired, supplemented with spontaneous outbreaks of baa-ing, something I found a little unnerving. I look forward to being met at away grounds with the sound of clinking tea cups on saucers.

If anything, Town had grown from the previous league encounter and, instead of hanging on, should have won the game, thus substituting a long fruitless journey to North Wales with a trip to the seaside.

As Leesley arrowed over a high, looping cross two minutes into injury time, my old self would have bet my house on Beck heading it in, as he towered above the Welsh defence. It's just as well I'm more sensible now.

It's now full time in north Wales. Town played well without scoring again and the brilliant 43 away fans out sang the Wrexham fans again, but our Cup run's over before it even started. Great credit must go to the Club for arranging free match tickets for the diehards on the coach, however, as I put the kettle on, I'm not envying them the long journey home.

As one fan, trying to put a brave face on it, wrote on Facebook, *'Who wanted to go to Weston-super-Mare anyway?'* Well I can tell you, I most definitely did.

Town bury Barrow, and I remember to put my shoes on before leaving home

Dagenham & Redbridge (A) L 1-2. Goal: Leesley. Crowd: 1,446. Barrow AFC (H) W 4-2. Goals: o.g., Muldoon, Falkingham, Beck. Crowd: 1,268. Article originally published on Thursday 1st November 2018 under the title 'No Groundhog Day as Town storm back for Barrow success.'

Groundhog Day: 'a situation in which a series of unwelcome events appear to be recurring in exactly the same way.'

It was half-time and Town were one nil down, it may have been two, to a team in blue and white. Just as I thought things couldn't get any worse, I glanced down at my feet to see that I'd turned up to the match in my slippers.

Then my alarm went off and it was 8am on Sunday morning.

I wasn't sure whether to be happy that the nightmare was at an end, or sad that I'd never know whether we managed to turn it around. One thing was certain though, losing to Dagenham and Redbridge in the unlucky manner that we did was thoroughly playing on my mind.

The trouble is, here I was watching the nightmare repeat itself on a bitterly cold Tuesday night at home to Barrow.

It had all started so positively. I'd made sure I had my shoes on before leaving the house with Molly, and Town had torn into the Cumbrians with all the intent of a team keen on erasing the bad memory of the weekend. Unfortunately this lasted for all of three minutes, as the visitors snapped at our midfield and grew into the game, whilst previously composed Town players resorted to long balls up field to the opposition goalkeeper and passes back to Belshaw.

When we went one down, I felt the same sinking feeling and wondered whether I really was stuck in Groundhog Day.

This time though, it was Town that woke up. Oh to have been a fly on the wall in the dressing room at half-time. A completely different team came out for the second half, playing a high pressing line against a team that liked to play out from the back, getting in behind the visitors' defence time and time again. Town were completely unplayable for fifteen glorious second half minutes and four goals.

Joe Leesley was again slinging in undefendable crosses from the left, and I was thrilled to see Mark Beck get on the end of one and ripple the net this week.

Two years ago Town were the underdogs when drawn at home against Barrow in the FA Trophy. The club gave the entire Wetherby Road stand to the visiting fans that day and only a couple of hundred turned up. This time, the visiting fans were given the quarter of the stand in which the vocal Town support stands when attacking the 1919 end of the ground. This led to the unusual sight of the Kop decamping en masse to the tiny 'Shed End' outside the Club Shop for the second half. It was a great atmosphere, but I'm not sure how many people will have seen the goals go in!

Don't you just love this rollercoaster game of football.

Print deadline met, it's now time for bed, and no work tomorrow. I think I'll set my alarm for 8.45am.

'Yes' he said, 'this is proper football.' Town burst the Chesterfield bubble

Chesterfield (H) D 1-1. Goal: Williams. Crowd: 2,291. Article originally published on Thursday 8th November 2018 under the title *'Deserted by my daughter during 'proper' clash with fallen giant.'*

I had this column all mapped out in advance. I was going to write about myself and my daughter. It was going to be funny and insightful in equal parts. That was until she decided to bring her friend along for a first visit and head off around the other side of the ground.

It's probably my fault, because I took up a standing position in the Wetherby Road Stand right next to the vocal 'jumping up and down' element, and it was a bit too raucous for her friend. At least that's the reason I'm giving, as the alternative is too hard to contemplate.

Still, apart from being deserted by Molly, I could quite get used to this. Another bumper crowd was inside Wetherby Road to see Town take on the latest fallen 'giant', this time in the form of Chesterfield, who filled the Kop with a large, boisterous following, probably the best we've seen so far.

I spoke to a fellow fan at half-time, saying how I was enjoying the spectacle, irrespective of the result, and appreciating how far we'd come in such a short time. *'Yes.'* he said, *'this is proper football.'*

In truth, there hadn't been a lot to cheer in the first half, but the match was always absorbing and finely balanced. The Spireites had come to frustrate and did it very well without ever looking a threat themselves.

It all changed within twelve minutes of the second period, when the visitors took the lead with their only shot on target out of three. They then sat deeper, and this gave Town a little more space to build from the back. Still though, nothing was coming off for the home side in the final third, as passing moves consistently broke down.

Fed up of being Billy No Mates, I'd stood next to my mate Mark behind the away dug-out, watching Martin Allen, the Chesterfield manager, pacing up and down the touchline going berserk at his players. I really wanted to put a hand on his shoulder and tell him to take it easy for the good of his health. Heaven knows what he's like when his team are losing.

Anyway, as I said, it all changed. My Zen-like calm exited stage left. As the away fans bounced up and down and shook the net, I really wanted Town to burst that bubble.

The visitors played into our hands by dropping even deeper, their time wasting punished by seven additional minutes. I was now joined by my daughter as Town laid siege towards the visiting fans and, in an almighty goalmouth scramble, where Town seemed to be doing their utmost best not to put the ball in the net again, up popped Williams to smash it home with the last kick of the game. Bubble well and truly burst.

I could go on again about this marvellous rollercoaster game of football but, in all truth, the outcome was entirely predictable. Chesterfield had drawn their previous five; four of them finishing one-all.

Pretty vacant.
Twiddling my
thumbs for England

Article originally published on Thursday 15th November 2018 under the title *'Another weekend of twiddling my thumbs due to postponement.'*

As if it wasn't bad enough having to twiddle my thumbs and spend the afternoon in a sodden Leeds city centre last Saturday, due to Town having no match on FA Cup First Round day, the situation was further exacerbated by news of the postponement of Town's league trip to Maidenhead this coming Saturday.

Scrutiny of the club website offered up the following tantalising headline: *'Our upcoming fixture at Maidenhead due to be played on Saturday 17th November has been postponed as a result of international call-ups.'* And that was it. No further details given. None.

At this stage, allow me to digress. Like the late, great Ronnie Corbett, I promise to get there eventually.

In the summer, prior to the World Cup, I was sitting down with Gareth Southgate's driver (his daughter is friends with my daughter, before you ask) and we were talking about how the England manager wasn't afraid to play younger, less established players in the national team.

Casually, I dropped Jack Emmett's name into the conversation and said that Gareth could do worse than pop down to Wetherby Road and check him out.

I was naturally disappointed, of course, that my efforts had fallen on deaf ears and Emmett had been overlooked for the World Cup squad. I'm still convinced he'd have killed off Croatia in the first half of that ill-fated semi-final.

So, had Gareth finally seen the light and called our Jack up to demolish Croatia in the forthcoming meaningless UEFA Nations League match? And why hadn't I read about this in the media, as opposed to the furore over Wayne Rooney's call up against the USA on Thursday?

Even more intriguingly, had Town fans' chants of '*England England's No. 1*' earned James Belshaw a long overdue first cap?

Further research on the internet, however, left me sorely disappointed.

It turns out that Maidenhead have two midfielders turning out for tiny Montserrat (population 4,900) against the slightly larger Aruba in the North & Central CONCAF Nations League Qualifiers this weekend.

Nevertheless, I still live in hope of spotting the England boss down at Wetherby Road one day in the near future. Seeing as he lives in the Harrogate district and I bumped into him at Brimham Rocks a few years ago, it's entirely possible he may fancy a Tuesday night match at some stage, if his chosen Premier League match is postponed. I mean, it's not as if he watches much football in his spare time...

If you do read this, Gareth, the fries and mushy peas are well worth checking out also.

We who wait. Anticipation, as Salford approaches

Article originally published on Thursday 22nd November 2018 under the title *'Relishing fixture congestion after three long weeks without a game.'*

As anyone of a certain age will tell you, life seems to pass you by much faster as you get older. Under normal circumstances, I'd agree wholeheartedly with this diagnosis, but these last three weeks with no Town game have dragged big time.

Now, sort of like the buses, you wait three weeks for a match to come along and then five turn up in two weeks. Six, if you count the West Riding County Cup match against near neighbours Guiseley on the Monday night.

To this end, I was glad to see Michael Woods return to Town in midweek. We're going to need the entire squad for the approaching fixture pile-up and another body in midfield will auger well going forward.

The big one for me and my daughter has to be the trip on the supporter's coach to Salford City on Tuesday night. You won't need reminding that they beat us twice last year, and that made up the six points difference between the two teams at the end of the season.

Around 250 supporters travelled to Salford in January, complete with a barrage of yellow and black balloons, only to see the team go in 2-0 down at half-time on a predictably rain-soaked Greater Manchester pitch. Town had seen a lot of good possession, but had struggled to get past the half way line and threaten the opposition goal as they battled the heavy pitch. Salford had just employed the tactic of pinging the ball into a slippery penalty area at every opportunity and seeing what chaos ensued.

The second half, however, was total one way traffic towards the travelling fans, as Town sought to turn the match around with urgent, incisive passing football. They managed to pull one back through Knowles just after the hour mark, but fell just short, deserving of at least a draw as the home fans bit their nails. I remember going home on the coach feeling gutted that we hadn't managed to equalise, but proud of the football Town had played that day, bolstered by non-stop encouragement from the travelling fans.

It almost goes without saying that both players and fans need to show that spirit again for the full ninety minutes on Tuesday night, as we seek to avenge last season.

But first, we have the not-so-little matter of lowly Braintree at Wetherby Road on Saturday. The Essex club have been dire on their home turf but slightly better on the road, and I'm hoping a rested team can avoid the kind of stuttering performance we put in against struggling Dover. It's often said that good things come to those that wait. In this case, let's certainly hope so.

(Greater) Manchester, so much to answer for. An x-rated night out in Salford

Braintree Town (H) W 3- 1. Goals: Muldoon, Thomson, Woods. Crowd: 1,454. Salford City (A) L 2-3. Goals: Muldoon, Kitching. Crowd: 1,200. Article originally published on Thursday 29th November 2018 under the title *Few comforting notes from a wet Tuesday night.'*

'Are you still planning to go to Salford on Tuesday?' enquires my wife on Sunday.

'Yes,' I say.

'Well Molly can't go with you,' comes her reply.

'Why? I thought we'd said she could have the one late night?' I protest, knowing full well I've already paid for her on the coach.

'She's got an appointment with the Orthodontist at ten to six.'

The coach leaves at five from outside the ground. And I've forgotten to cancel said appointment.

On long family journeys in the car, we often play a game where each person has to name an item based around a chosen subject for each letter of the alphabet. We normally struggle on *'x'*. Last time my daughter chose *'the things dad's forgotten'* as the subject matter. When we got to *'n'*, my wife said *'nearly everything'* and Molly asked if we could stop playing, as it was far too easy. But persevere we did, and I claimed a victory, of sorts, when they couldn't think of anything beginning with *'x'*.

Anyhow, one grovelling Monday morning call to the Orthodontist's to rearrange the appointment later, my daughter and I find ourselves boarding one of two supporters' club coaches on a bitterly cold and wet Harrogate evening. It's so cold and wet that even the dog refuses to go out. I find myself questioning my sanity.

After a not so quick journey on the four lane car park, also known as the M62 in rush hour, we arrive in Salford.

It's the same brand new stadium as last season, built seemingly out of Meccano (youngsters ask your parents). Even the terraces are metal. But there seem to be fewer home fans. A study of the attendance figures after the fact reveals a 700 plus drop on last season, there can't have been more than a thousand home fans there to see a team on a fifteen game unbeaten run. Then it hits me, Manchester United are at home in the Champions League.

A noisy, sizeable following cheers Town on and the players seem to respond, twice taking the lead and looking dangerous every time they go forward. Unfortunately we fail to nail home the advantage when we have the home side on the ropes before half-time. To their credit, Salford also look dangerous going forward. It's been a belter of an end-to-end first half, and one of the best I've ever seen. Town really should be leading 6-4 at half-time, but go in at two all.

Salford then mug us with a free kick routine twelve minutes into the second half before falling back and defending in numbers for the last half an hour. Town have the bulk of the possession but, just like last January, can't find a way through the massed ranks, as the referee does his level best to ignore endless pulling of Beck's shirt in the area. Again. For the umpteenth match running.

Woods comes on, but can't get close to repeating THAT goal against Braintree on Saturday. An unbelievable goal that got so much exposure on the TV and internet, that five people came up to me at work in Leeds to talk about it.

This is the first time Molly's seen us lose since Blyth Spartans last season, as she missed Leyton Orient at home due to a friend's birthday party. To almost compound our misery, the coach refuses to start for a while, and we contemplate a long night in Salford. Luckily, the driver works his magic and we make it back to Wetherby Road.

The only crumb of comfort I can find this Tuesday night is the fact that *'Orthodontist'* doesn't begin with *'x'*.

Dog bears brunt
of Solihull mishap

Maidenhead United (A) W 2-1. Goals: Howe, Langmead. Crowd: 1,090. Solihull Moors (A) L 0-2. Crowd: 794. Article originally published on Thursday 6th December 2018 under the title *'Dog bears brunt of Solihull mishap'* (I'm stealing that one).

'It's gone in, Town have scored!' yells an excited Barry Parker on Radio York.

'Yes!!' I jump up throwing the dog into the air. Accidentally of course.

But, no, wait a minute...

'Has it gone in?' enquires an unsure Parker... *'No, it's hit the stanchion.'*

'Grrrr!' That's me, not the dog.

And that, I'm afraid, was the high point of an out of character performance at Solihull on Tuesday night.

Oh, the 'joy' of listening to the radio. Still, it could be worse. I could actually have made the long journey down there to watch a lacklustre Town display.

You see, I'd booked Tuesday and Wednesday off work intending to visit my dad in the West Midlands. This was before my wife pointed out that I really should go on a weekend, so Molly could travel down with me to see grandad. Of course, I couldn't argue against this superior logic and had to postpone. The fact that Town were at Solihull Moors on the Tuesday night had nothing to do with my plans, of course, it was just pure coincidence. And even if it wasn't, I really couldn't make that argument.

A few frustrations boiled over online after the match, but it seems like it was just a game too far, in a week of three tough away trips, for our small squad.

Taking the wider view, this is probably the first time the players haven't really turned up in the league this season, and the frustration speaks volumes for how well we've done so far and the expectations heaped onto a newly promoted team.

Looking at the statistics, our glass ceiling is there for all to see. We've played eight competitive matches against teams in the current top six and won only one, failing to score in six.

If we're to progress in the National League, it's this lack of penetration against the teams around us that we need to address. We haven't been outclassed by anyone, but the players need to learn to adopt the clinical nature in front of goal that Leyton Orient displayed when they visited Wetherby Road earlier in the season.

Perversely, whilst Town are second top scorers in the league, two behind Salford, they've also conceded the most goals of any team in the top half of the table. Wrexham are level with us despite scoring seventeen goals fewer, due to the tightness of their defence. Saying that, I wouldn't have it any other way. We've certainly seen some thrills and spills following Town, and I hope I've reflected that excitement in my column. Like Town, once or twice, I feel I've been off the pace, but I've tried my utmost to convey the sense of a wonderful journey into the unknown.

So, with Aldershot at home on Saturday and the juicy prospect of York City in the FA Trophy the following

Saturday, grandad's just going to have to wait until the Saturday before Christmas to see his grand-daughter.

Warren doesn't miss
a (hat)trick

Aldershot Town (H) W 4-1. Goals: Burrell 3, Muldoon. Crowd: 1,362.
Article originally published on Thursday 13th December 2018 under
the title *'Burrell treble rubs salt into the wounds for travelling fans.'*

'Aldershot, Alder-shot!'

With all the Kop to choose from, Molly and I elect to stand
behind the two most annoying away fans you're ever likely to
meet. It's hard to concentrate on the match when the bloke in
front is bouncing up and down with his back to the pitch,
drunkenly singing out-of tune songs towards the home fans.

One of them catches the ball after their keeper palms a
Thomson shot past the post and dances about wildly with it.

'Good catch, eh?' he whispers to Molly, as she flashes him a
long-suffering smile.

My daughter thinks the blokes in front are funny, but I've
just about had enough. The straw that breaks the camel's
back is the fact that Town are one down.

It's been said that tact is the ability to tell someone to go
to hell in such a way that they look forward to the trip. So I
politely, but firmly, inform the bloke in front that Aldershot
are playing in the exact opposite direction to which he's
looking.

To his credit, he calms down, apologises and says that he's
in Harrogate mainly for an enjoyable weekend away as his
team are rubbish. As if to then prove his point, Warren
Burrell equalises in front of us.

At half-time, the home choir leaves the Aldershot fans in the Kop and heads down to the Club Shop end for the second half. It worked against Barrow, when Town crashed in four in fifteen minutes, and it works again today. Normal service is resumed, and a great second half performance sees three more goals, with Burrell completing a popular, yet unlikely, hat trick.

The first three goals all arrive via the same source. A Joe Leesley set-piece and a Burrell finish; two great headers and a goalmouth scramble finish, following a header. The fourth goal from Muldoon is pure route one, direct from a James Belshaw assist.

It's no small irony, that for all our pass and move football, a feature of our season so far has been the amount of important goals contributed by Howe, Langmead and Kitching from set-piece situations, admittedly set-piece situations won as a result of our nice football. Warren must have been feeling left out.

With Orient, Salford and Solihull all dropping points, Town are back up into third, top scorers in the league and four points off the top. I reckon three more points should see us safe from relegation. Can we do it by Christmas?

'Dad? Can your toes actually fall off?'

York City (H) W 2-1 (FA Trophy First Round). Goals: Knowles, Kitching. Crowd: 1,336. Article originally published on Thursday 20th December 2018 under the title *'York success shows just how far we've come.'*

It's ten minutes into a bitterly cold second half against York City in the FA Trophy.

'Dad?' says Molly.

'Yes?' I reply, tentatively.

'Can your toes actually fall off?' she enquires.

Now, I must admit I didn't see that one coming.

I could have dealt with questions such as *'Can I have some chips?'* and *'Why do all the players bunch up to one side of the pitch when the goalkeeper takes a goal kick?'* Well, we'd already had the chips, and the goal kick situation is a mystery to everyone I talk to, but you get my point.

We're stood in the Kop with the Town fans, freezing sleet lashing into our faces, toes frozen, and I can totally see where my daughter's coming from.

'Don't be daft,' I reply.

In truth, it had taken me a while to cotton on to the weather conditions. My brain normally associates foul weather at football matches with a mud bath of a pitch, yet here we were watching football on a pristine 3G surface.

It's only when surface water started becoming apparent, and Molly initially refused to come out of a very cosy 1919

[62]

bar for the second half, that I realised just how bad it was out there.

The first half had seen a muted Town display facing into the driving wind and rain, with York having played the conditions well to cause us one or two problems. We gifted them a goal, and were lucky not to concede again, before equalising and then missing a sitter ourselves.

The anticipated atmosphere had been muted by the weather too. The attendance was less than half of the turnout for the glorious derby in the National League North last year and fans huddled into the stands, staying clear of the front rows, and certainly clear of any uncovered areas of the ground. Water cascaded down from the Shed End roof and the sleet was freezing on contact with the ground.

Town came out and really turned the screw in the second half though, dominating the ball with the weather behind them. Yet for all the possession and half chances, we were grateful, once again, to defender Liam Kitching for lashing a loose ball high into the rain sodden net.

So, victory over our neighbours for the third time in three matches was secured, cementing Town's position as the pride of North Yorkshire in the process. Who would have dreamt of that when the visitors were in the old Division Two?

Seeing York play really drove it home as to how far Town have progressed in the last year. To these eyes, at times they looked every inch an average National League North team, and a notch below most other opponents we've seen at Wetherby Road this season. That Town have stepped up to the higher level so well is a credit to everyone involved with the club.

I'd like to report that fans and players celebrated long and hard after the final whistle, but in truth, I've never seen players move so fast for the dressing rooms, as we and half the Kop dashed for the warmth of home and a chance to check that toes were all present and correct.

It was a very strange local derby indeed.

Radio silence

Eastleigh (A) L 1-2. Goal: Leesley. Crowd: 1,622. Article originally published on Thursday 27th December 2018 under the title *'Disappointed to miss chance to go second.'*

Earlier in the season, I wrote about the tribulations of attempting to follow Town via a dodgy Radio York reception in a Halifax car park. This week, I didn't even have the comfort of that, as I was on a bus with Molly in the Midlands whilst Town were kicking off at Eastleigh.

My daughter's phone pinged with news of a goal for Leesley inside two minutes and high fives were exchanged, much to the bemusement of fellow passengers, as we thought we were in for a good afternoon. Radio York online was only broadcasting the York match so, on searching for National League commentaries, the BBC directed me to Radio Solent. Result!

I excitedly found the commentary page, clicked and was met with... *'This programme is currently unavailable.'* Even though it would probably have been Southampton on there if I could have accessed it anyway, the BBC has diminished in my eyes.

On arriving at my dad's to find Sky Sports on loud enough for the neighbours to enjoy it, Town had been pegged back, but it was a luxury to have rolling National League updates on there.

Now, as any fan watching for score updates from long distance will tell you, the long period of 'silence' when nothing happens is almost as much torture as being at the match itself.

Salford, Orient and Solihull all conceded, but there was nothing from Eastleigh. Yet. The script was being written, I lived in hope. Then *'Eastleigh 2 Harrogate Town 1'* rolled into view in the 82nd minute. I blinked, surely they had that the wrong way round? Unfortunately, no correction was forthcoming.

My mood wasn't lightened by Twitter informing me that Thomson had had a shot cleared off the line. To rub salt into the wound, Orient had scored twice.

We would have gone joint-second with a win. It seems like it was a hard fought match that could have gone either way, and I'll definitely take fourth at Christmas. Yet, the concern is that we've lost the last four out of five on our travels, having been undefeated away in the first eight. Luckily, our home form remains consistent.

If my memory serves me correctly, Town set a similar early pace last season before hitting a rocky spell on their travels around Christmas, losing at Darlington, Spennymoor and Salford amongst others. They pulled it around then, and I hope that experience will stand us in good stead this season.

Will anyone be able to keep pace with Leyton Orient? Are they due a rough spell soon? Or are we all vying for the play off positions? Only time will tell.

Christmas deadlines and all that, I'm having to write this before the matches over the festive period. Let's hope a large Boxing Day Halifax crowd sees a Town reaction.

One thing's for certain, I won't be following it from any car park.

What could possibly go wrong?

FC Halifax Town (H) L 1- 2. Goal: Howe. Crowd: 2,310. AFC Fylde (H) L 1- 2. Goal: Beck. Crowd: 1,603. Article originally published on Thursday 3rd January 2019 under the title *'Helter-skelter ride continues apace, but luck needs to turn.'*

I was chatting with a colleague at work recently, describing how I was approaching Town's maiden National League season as a glorious, helter-skelter ride into the unknown. *'That's all very well and good,'* he said whilst stepping into the lift, *'but your team hasn't hit a bad spell yet.'*

It's Boxing Day and I'm excited.

I ask Molly if she's going to wear her santa hat to the match, and my daughter flashes me a look of abject pity. *'But it's Christmas and there'll be loads of people wearing them,'* I protest.

There's a large crowd expected. Town have lost at home only once all season. The visitors, Halifax, have won only once in eighteen league games since August. What could possibly go wrong?

Well to start with, the fixture is segregated and Halifax fans are given the entire Wetherby Road stand, which they then proceed to only half-fill; something that's not altogether surprising given their current form. Hindsight says the smaller Kop would have been the better choice for away fans, as per Wrexham and Chesterfield, due to the 2,310 crowd containing a brilliant turnout of nearly 1,900 home fans.

[67]

This means that when Molly and I arrive twenty minutes before kick-off, the Town areas of the ground are already pretty much full with displaced Wetherby Road regulars. We choose to settle for the position where we watched our first match from, behind the wall in front of the hospitality area. We have to, as it's the only space we can find at the front.

Looking around, I count only four others in santa hats beside myself. All are young children, three are in the away end. The omens don't look good.

Town score the opening goal for the first time in six home matches, bizarrely the previous five had seen four home wins and a score draw, and go in one up at half-time. The normally boisterous Town choir is split between the Kop and the 'Shed End' and I look forward to the second half with Town attacking a reunited noisy Kop end. However Town don't turn up second half and Halifax deservedly snatch the points. The atmosphere becomes subdued, as the players don't give us much to cheer, but the Halifax fans find their voices with the late winner and celebrate as if they've won the league.

Fylde at home sees a déjà vu moment, except thankfully there's no segregation and the visitors score first this time through a Danny Rowe thunderbolt.

I'd already warned Molly about Rowe in the first half, when he almost snapped the cross bar in two, but she wasn't impressed, saying he'd had three chances and missed them all. *'I'm worried he's just finding his range,'* I'd replied. It gives me no joy to say that, for once, I was right.

At risk of raising my blood pressure, the officials are shocking. Constant shirt pulling on Beck in the area goes unpunished again, whilst a Fylde player falling over as Falkingham brushes past him results in a penalty.

'2-0, it's Rowe,' I state. *'I think he'll miss it,'* says Molly.

Belshaw's penalty save galvanises Town and they claw their way back into it. You can't fault the effort. I'd have taken the point, but we're undone by another refereeing decision in stoppage time. Whether it was a foul tackle or not is debatable, but having studied the highlights almost to the point of insanity, nothing will convince me that their striker breaking through was onside. Head in hands, I catch the eyes of the Fylde fan next to me. He smiles in sympathy.

Up steps Rowe again. Like I said, he was just finding his range.

So, we've suffered two late defeats in matches that could have ended differently on another day. And therein lies the crux of the problem. Town are playing well enough in spells, but we're seeing less of that high-pressing, run-at-the-opposition-and-cause-mayhem approach as displayed so well in the opening match against Sutton. Passes that would previously have been played purposely through midfield are going backwards or being lumped hopefully forwards. Those little triangles on the wing to get the player in behind, and the lung-busting, gambling runs into the area to get on the end of the subsequent cross aren't happening with as much frequency.

This shouldn't come as a shock really. We're no longer the surprise package and the teams we're playing are a step up in quality from last year. They've done their homework and seen how we play.

We also need our luck to turn.

So although he may be right about the bad spell, my work colleague is only partially correct. I'm still treating Town's maiden National League season as a helter-skelter ride into the unknown, albeit a little less gloriously this week.

Molly at The Shay, August 2016. Her first away trip to watch Town.

Half time at Southport on a filthy Tuesday night, September 2017.

**Southport fans brave the elements to see their team
crash 4-1 to Town, September 2017.**

**Jack Emmett runs at the York City defence during Town's
2-0 victory, in the first competitive meeting of the two
North Yorkshire clubs, September 2017.** *(Mike Worsley)*

At home in the Wetherby Road Stand, next to a flat-capped
Johnny Walker, Town's longest serving fan. Bradford Park Avenue
are the visitors in the FA Cup, September 2017. *(Mike Worsley)*

Town fans and players celebrating a goal during the 3-2 victory
at Darlington in the FA Trophy, November 2017. *(Matt Kirkham)*

Away at Salford City, January 2018. Town went down 2-1, but both teams went on to win promotion from the National League North.

FC of Manchester United manage to keep this one out in front of the Kop, March 2018. Town ran out 6-0 winners.

**Warren Burrell heads away in front of the travelling support
at Bootham Crescent, York City, April 2018.** *(Matt Kirkham)*

Jake Wright on his way to scoring the first goal in the 2-0 victory.

Ryan Fallowfield leads the celebrations. *(Matt Kirkham)*

A section of the travelling support, as Molly looks out for me.

Joy and disbelief in the Wetherby Road Stand at the end of the Chorley Play-Off Semi-Final May 2018. *(Matt Kirkham)*

A hug for Simon Weaver, whilst Jordan Ford celebrates, Chorley Play-Off Semi-Final May 2018. *(Matt Kirkham)*

Joe Leesley (out of picture) scores the third goal against Brackley Town in the National League North Play-Off Final. *(Mike Worsley)*

**Leesley celebrating at the end in front of the Kop.
Note the lack of segregation in a capacity crowd.** *(Matt Kirkham)*

Foreground left to right: Lloyd Kerry, James Belshaw (with trophy), Josh Falkingham, Ryan Fallowfield, Warren Burrell (with champagne) and Simon Weaver celebrating winning the National League North Play-Off Final. *(Matt Kirkham)*

Our first National League away day at Victoria Park, Hartlepool, August 2018. Town came away with a deserved two-all draw.

New Year's Day, fond memories of Halifax, and two points lost

FC Halifax Town (A) D 1-1. Goal: Thomson. Crowd: 1,696. Sutton United (A) L 1-2. Goal: Thomson. Crowd: 1,841. Article originally published on Thursday 10th January 2019 under the title *'Why attack is the best form of defence.'*

It's New Year's Day and after being fed and watered by the grandparents, Molly and I take a fifteen minute stroll down to FC Halifax's ground.

I've fond memories of attending The Shay on distant Friday nights, when the cosy main Skircoat Stand used to be half wooden seats, half standing and the away end was a cinder bank, separated from the pitch by a speedway track. Salubrious it wasn't, but it was a great place to occasionally watch football along with the fifteen hundred or so regulars.

Nowadays it's a smart new 14,000 capacity stadium. Only the Skircoat Stand remains from the old days, sadly all-seated and closed today, as is the terraced Hunger Hill Stand to the right of us, its forlorn crash barriers draped with banners. 235 Town fans are allotted a third of the main all-seated stand, whilst 1,461 Halifax fans spread out in the other two thirds, plus the stand behind the goal, albeit confined to three sections out of the five available.

'Wish we had a ground like this,' comments someone behind us. It's a fair point, but I'd miss the homeliness and

atmosphere of Wetherby Road and the ability to watch the match from all parts of the ground.

'Your ground's too big for you,' chant the Town fans, not unreasonably, trying their hardest to get some kind of atmosphere going.

In fact, I'm surprised Halifax manage to break into four figures these days considering the admission prices. £20 for me and £9 for Molly is just plain unreasonable. Grandad tells us before the game of a disused tunnel into the ground from the adjacent bus station and how fans used it to gain access into the old ground without paying. Urban myth or not, I'd like to find it today.

Molly has fond memories of attending The Shay a couple of years ago, when we ran out 1-0 winners with an Emmett worldie of a goal, although I think Lloyd Kerry would choose to forget it, the home fans booing him for time-wasting as he walked off with a fractured cheek bone and eye socket. Both are playing today.

I don't recall seeing a more one-sided first half in a long time. The home team are forced to sit deep, chasing shadows, as Town camp in their half playing some great pressing and passing football. The players look really hungry and up for it. Town should be one up after twenty seconds and actually do go one up after five minutes from an attempted cross. Of course Thomson meant it! We should be three up at half-time, but go in at just one.

That Halifax are still in the match is due to the fact that, for all our great football, we seem to be carving out very few clear scoring opportunities. Players seem reticent to shoot, choosing to overplay on the edge of the area. Too much of the passing is in front of our opponents and there's a lack of numbers in the area when Leesley and Thomson do ping it in there. I'm personally not keen on the 4-5-1 formation. It means we gain strength in midfield but lose out upfront with strikers sat on the bench. Add to that, the inability to clinically finish the two or three great chances we do create, and we have the recipe for a nail-biting second half.

Molly has £10 from grandad burning a hole in her pocket, so we disappear under the stand for chips and coffee. I need some sustenance as I can't help feeling that the home team can't possibly play that badly for another forty five minutes.

They don't, but we look fairly comfortable for much of the second period without creating much and, when Halifax do get sight of goal, their shooting is woeful. The last ten minutes sees the Shaymen lay siege to the Town goal though. We look tired and panicked, dropping too deep and hacking the ball away in the vague vicinity of an isolated Beck, only for Halifax to pump it straight back in. It's cruel, but no surprise when they score late. It's definitely two points lost and the players look dejected as they come over to thank us for the support.

The hope that this is the end of our losing streak is cruelly dashed at Sutton. Again, Town dictate the game in midfield, but an inability to turn the dominance into more than one, whilst conceding two, proves to be the current Achilles' heel.

Earlier on in the season, if our opponents scored two, we scored three. Personally, I'd like to see us get back to that. Attack is the best form of defence in my humble opinion, and the last ten minutes at Halifax shows that we can't sit deep and defend.

I'll leave you all to debate that one.

Maybe our luck is slowly starting to change

Dover Athletic (A) W 2-1 (FA Trophy Second Round). Goals: Muldoon 2. Crowd: 463. Article originally published on Thursday 17th January 2019 under the title *'Win at Dover has given us all a boost.'*

I think it's fair to say that the FA Trophy win at Dover Athletic has buoyed us all. It wasn't only the result, but the strong manner of the performance that was so pleasing, bearing in mind that Dover were on a run of four wins and a draw in the last six matches, having turned over Wrexham the week before. For me, it's up there with one of the best wins of the season.

Hats off to the minibus load of Town fans who made the long trek down to deepest Kent at the weekend to cheer the team on and sang their hearts out.

'Make plenty of noise guys. Want to hear you on Radio York!' was one comment on the Town Facebook Supporters' page pre-match.

It seems they took it literally, as a few of them went into the main stand to serenade match commentator Barry Parker, much to the bemusement of the Radio Kent commentators and the enjoyment of those of us listening at home on the radio.

The big news from the match in Kent though is that we were awarded our first penalty since Knowles put one away at Gateshead and, I think, only our second of the season. Maybe our luck is slowly starting to change. Or maybe we found a decent referee for once. Unfortunately, we didn't have a regular penalty taker on the pitch, with both Leesley and Knowles not starting. Never mind, I'll keep shouting for them every time Beck's shirt gets pulled in the area. You never know.

Despite the recent run of results, I maintain there's not that much wrong with the way Town are playing and the confidence of the squad is high. In fact, we've been bossing the majority of the recent games in midfield, but not hammering our possession advantage home.

As I stated in these very pages last week, I think it's all about a little bit more positivity in and around the opposition penalty area, making those penetrating runs behind the defence, and players getting into scoring positions. It was good to see Jack Muldoon back in the team and benefitting from two near post finishes by doing exactly that at Dover. Add to that a solid defensive performance and, penalty miss aside, it made for the perfect performance.

Well done to Harrogate Town Ladies for a great 3-2 win over a strong Hartlepool United Ladies team last Sunday. Let's hope the men can repeat that performance in the Saturday lunchtime clash. It's sold out and Hartlepool fans have the Wetherby Road Stand again, so Molly and I are going to have to arrive almost at the crack of dawn to get a good vantage point in front of the BT Sport cameras.

Television personalities

Hartlepool United (H) W 3-1. Goals: Kerry, Muldoon, Beck. Crowd: 2,000. Article originally published on Thursday 24th January 2019 under the title *'Town hit top form in front of TV cameras.'*

It's 11:30, still an hour and five minutes to kick off, and we're firmly planted behind a crash barrier in a barely quarter full Kop. It's a little earlier than planned, I thought kick off was at 12:15, but at least we've got a good vantage point as it's going to be packed today.

We amuse ourselves by spotting TV cameras, predicting the score, eating our way through our half-time snacks and watching the players warm up in front of us, shadowed by the obligatory cameraman. I'd have liked to have killed ten minutes reading the programme, but they sold out just as we entered. Sort it out Town!

There's a pitch side camera in front of us and, right on cue, the sprinklers flick on in the goalmouth and douse the cameraman and a gaggle of young kids at the front with freezing water. *'Welcome to Yorkshire!'* shouts someone behind me.

The youngsters, barely tall enough to see over the railings at the front, jump up and down and wave as the cameraman points his camera towards them. *'I'm Harrogate's biggest fan!'* shouts one of them, waving his scarf over his head. *'No, I am!'* retorts another. They remind me of my early years watching Wolves and the buzz of excitement I always felt when the cameras were at Molineux. I wonder whether it's the same for Molly. *'Not really,'* says my grown up daughter.

Town look up for it pre-match. Hartlepool don't even seem able to pull their socks up properly, until I realise that the insipid, flesh coloured trim on top of the red just makes it appear like that.

The Town players go for the jugular from the off and this time get the early goal, Kerry's sheer persistence and positivity to get into the area paying off. The visitors look shell-shocked, bullied out of possession when they get it, and unable to live with Town's attacking intent. Sometimes first impressions can be telling.

Then something extraordinary happens. The referee awards a penalty for shirt pulling on Beck. Stunned silence. We miss for the second time in a week, but it's a great save from the Pools' keeper, hard and low to his right.

We go in 1-0 up at half-time, but it should be more. Please don't let this be another Halifax, I think. It turns out I'll have no need to worry.

Half-time entertainment is provided by two local youngsters' teams taking penalties in front of a sizeable audience in the Kop. Even their coaches can't resist a penalty each. I find myself wondering who's enjoying it the most.

Early in the second half, Thomson picks up the ball in midfield, drives forward and hits a low shot. It's not hard enough to beat the keeper, and the chance looks to have gone as the parry out evades a lurking Beck. Quick as a flash Kerry pounces, nicks the ball off a dithering defender, touches it to Muldoon and CRACK! Beck takes evasive action and I swear twenty people behind the goal duck with him, as the ball crashes into the back of the net and back out again. Blink and you missed it. It's goal of the season for me. Yes, Woods' strike against Braintree included. Five minutes later, Molly receives a screenshot from her friend. She's been spotted celebrating on BT Sport.

Hartlepool steal a goal back against the run of play, but Town aren't going to let this one slip. Another penetrating run from Muldoon pays off as he gets behind the defence, crosses, and Beck loops an inch perfect header over the keeper. It's a well deserved reward for the striker's best performance in a Town shirt, having bullied the visitors defence all afternoon, sorry, lunchtime.

What a brilliant performance. I think it's safe to say that Town have their mojo well and truly back.

My only grumble? I predicted the score as 4-1, based on those alluded to first impressions, so I'm rueing the penalty miss.

Molly predicted 3-1.

Oblivious

Article originally published on Thursday 31st January 2019 under the title *'No action on the pitch, but plenty off it.'*

I'm writing this having just tuned into Barnet v Brentford in the FA Cup on Radio 5, the reason for Town not having a match this week. It was a breathless, seesaw cup tie which ended three goals apiece in front of a raucous crowd, the BBC commentators almost giddy with excitement at times. Afterwards, they express surprise at the quality of football played by a team from the fifth tier. Maybe they should get out more.

I relate the score to my daughter Molly. She already knows, of course, as she receives all the National League teams' score updates on her mobile. We can't go anywhere on a match day without nuggets such as *'Maidenhead are winning one nil at Braintree, Dad.'*

There may not have been any action on the pitch Town-wise but it's certainly all go off it, with works underway for no less than three new stands to satisfy a National League requirement that all newly promoted teams should have a ground capacity of at least 4,000 by 31st March if they wish to stay in the league and take part in the play-offs. A statement of intent indeed and exciting times to be a Town fan. Maybe also an admission from the club that we're safe from relegation!

It means that the capacity will be reduced in the short term to around 2,000, but the club has the timing just about right as all the teams with large followings have already visited Wetherby Road in the league, and we now entertain a run of southern clubs, with the exception of Salford.

This coming Saturday sees Stockport County make the journey to Wetherby Road in the FA Trophy. Last year, an unstoppable Town put four past them on a Tuesday night, yet I was utterly gutted for days. I know that may sound all wrong, but I wasn't there to witness one of the best displays of the season. Neither was Molly. It was the only home match we missed all season and, to compound the misery, Jack Emmett scored a stunner.

Thanks for your concern, dear reader, but I wasn't ill. Neither was I on holiday, at work or visiting relatives. I was a few hundred yards away at home, under the impression that it was Monday, blissfully unaware of the glow from the floodlights outside my front window. It wasn't until I switched the computer on at 10pm that night, that I realised my grave error.

If only Molly had signed up to National League score updates back then, we'd have realised when the first goal went in and rushed over there.

'Man of the match?'
'Who's left on the bench?'

Stockport County (H) L 2-4 (FA Trophy Third Round), Goals: o.g.,
Thomson. Crowd: 1,142. Article originally published on Thursday
7th February 2019 under the title *'Home defence lets us down in
Trophy loss.'*

As the fourth goal goes in and the Stockport fans wave
goodbye to a mini exodus of Town fans from the Kop, I must
admit that I hadn't seen that one coming at twenty past
three.

Wind back seventy five minutes and, the absence of
cameras apart, we could still be at the Hartlepool match two
weeks previously. It's the same starting line-up and the
Wetherby Road regulars have again been ousted into the Kop.
Town are one nil up attacking the Building Site End and
seemingly in control against another ex-League club.

There's one other important absence though, in my eyes,
as the players seem to be lacking the same high intensity and
sharpness they'd displayed so handsomely in front of the Sky
viewers.

Sure enough, we gift Stockport two chances in three crazy
minutes through loose passing across our back line, and the
wheels come off. The first goal leads to an outpouring of
frustration from Belshaw, having got a hand to the low shot,
and some rather choice words that I shan't repeat in polite
company. Following the second, defenders start arguing
amongst themselves. Town have lost their heads and a

buoyed Stockport take advantage, running riot down our left flank.

Town manage to reach half-time without conceding again and could even have levelled if they'd shown the same clinical finishing as the visitors when put through on goal.

'Never mind,' Molly says, 'the manager will have a word at half-time.' What he most certainly didn't say is 'gift them another goal from a back pass inside three minutes of the restart.' Well, at least I hope he didn't.

From then on, Town huff and puff without much success, creating two or three decent chances but failing to set up the craved-for grandstand finish. Williams has an improvised effort cleared off the line. We jump up, thinking it's in.

Stockport seem happy to pack their half, soak up pressure, watch us pass in front of them and then pick us off. The visitors' tactics bear fruit again when home defenders go on a kamikaze mission forward. We lose the ball and one pass takes out the remnants of our back line, finding ex-Town man Mulhern alone in the centre circle and through on goal. He takes the ball past Belshaw, teases our defenders by watching them all run back madly towards the goal before turning, pausing, pausing again and then slotting the ball coolly into the net. Could things get any worse?

Gallows humour sets in amongst the spectators when the tannoy announcer declares the Harrogate Town 'Man Of The Match'. 'Who's left on the bench?' shouts one wag. My vote's for our new loanee left back, Jack Senior, as he's only been on the pitch for a few minutes and can't be held responsible. Let's hope he hasn't seen this performance and begs Luton to take him back.

Town finally manage to pull one back three minutes from time and, when the fourth official holds up four minutes on his board, Molly cheers and says *'That's good isn't it? We've still got time.'* Oh the boundless optimism of youth. I think he was taunting us with the score line.

Even though we've handed them four goals on a plate in a complete horrorshow of a performance, Stockport are the better team today. They're on the crest of a nine match winning run and it shows, as they play with all the verve Town displayed two weeks earlier. Sometimes, you just have to give some credit to the opposing team, learn from it and move on.

The one high spot is that I bump into an old allotment friend, John, who admits to reading this column every week. I hope this re-living of the nightmare hasn't put him off!

Dance, dance, dance, dance, dance to the radio.
You score two,
we'll score three!

Dover Athletic (A) W 3-2. Goals: o.g., Beck, Thomson. Crowd: 997.
Article originally published on Thursday 14th February 2019 under
the title *'Late winner keeps Town in play-off battle.'*

'Who wants a clean sheet? They're boring!'

Not my words, but the words of an over excited Barry
Parker on Radio York, if uttered slightly tongue in cheek as
he'd just spent most of the second half wondering whether
Town would keep their first clean sheet in seventeen
matches.

George Thomson had just won the game in the 92nd
minute with a *'super worldie'* and I'd bellowed the news out
excitedly to Molly upstairs whilst jumping around, beating
her phone's National League Score Update by some distance.

This was the perfect way to banish the memory of last
week's calamitous FA Trophy performance.

Yet there was no inkling of such a frantic ending to come,
as Town were pushed back in the second period, defending a
one goal lead from the seventh minute. So far the defence had
stood firm, with both Belshaw and Fallowfield performing
heroically, but you could sense it coming as Dover pressed for
an equaliser.

When Town fell behind in three unfortunate minutes, my heart sank, it felt like Sutton United all over again.

Town looked down and out, but this squad of players just don't know when they're beaten. The equaliser came via fresh legs, subs Mottley-Henry and Williams combining to provide Beck with a near post finish. And then came Thomson, turning and arcing in a shot from way out on the left wing.

After the match, Simon Weaver said that he thought the players had looked unusually fatigued, but perversely it was this fatigue that won the game in such thrilling fashion.

Describing his winning goal in a post match interview, Thommo said... *'I'll be honest. My legs had gone ... and it was just the first thing that came to my mind, I just need to get a strike off here.'*

I know the manager and many of you may not agree, but I think we've been worrying far too much over our inability to keep a clean sheet. Last time we kept one was in the goalless draw against Wrexham in November, admittedly an entertaining goalless draw, but overrated all the same. Don't get me wrong, I'd have happily taken a 1-0 at Dover, so would my dodgy heart, but the fans that made the long journey to the Crabble won't forget those crazy thirteen minutes in a long, long time.

So I have to declare that I'm with Barry, albeit tongue firmly out of cheek. You score two, we'll score three!

Defeat would have seen us starting to slide out of the play off positions, but now we find ourselves still in the thick of it, especially if we can make our game in hand pay. Only nine points separated the top nine before Tuesday and, with no team showing signs of wanting to run away with things, it's all to play for.

We are the men in black. A tale of two referees

Ebbsfleet United (H) L 1-2. Goal: Muldoon. Crowd: 1,488. Article originally published on Thursday 21st February 2019 under the title *'Sing when we are winning? Chance would be a fine thing.'*

It has all the makings of a good day.

There's a sizeable, expectant home crowd buoyed by the last minute win at Dover last week, hoping to cheer Town on to a straight third league win.

A surprisingly large away following is making itself heard in the tea bar side of the Wetherby Road stand pre-kick off, as fans of both teams happily mingle, even if one Ebbsfleet fan does try to steal one of my chips dipped in mushy peas. Town fans are also back in the Wetherby Road side and, with a run of home games against mainly southern teams and the new stands rising up, have we seen the end of the giving over of this part of the ground to large contingents of visiting fans? I, for one, hope so.

Twenty minutes in, I find myself checking the time, hoping that Town can get to half-time only the one goal down. And that's before the visitors hit the post twice in one attack. The only upside of conceding early is that we don't have to worry about keeping a clean sheet for another week. Ebbsfleet came into this game on the back of two successive league defeats. You'd never know. Best laid plans and all that.

The most excitement from a Town point of view is when the referee goes down with a pulled muscle and ends up substituting himself.

It's frustrating to watch, as Town find themselves second best to nearly everything, but the players rally, manage to get a foothold in the game, and are unlucky to equalise in a great fifteen minute attacking spell before half-time. When Muldoon slots in, following a sweeping move five minutes into the second half, all our frustrations pour out into a huge roar. Now, surely, the game's there for the taking.

The hoped-for Town blitzkrieg doesn't materialise however and, with the game a bit too open for my liking, I'm beginning to settle for a hard-earned point. If only.

Falkingham breaks through on goal and falls under a challenge. Home fans scream for a penalty. The substitute referee waves play on, before awarding Ebbsfleet a soft free kick in a dangerous location down the other end. Town defenders clear the first ball but completely fail to pick up two runners from the second as the ball hits the net in front of the disbelieving travelling fans.

The referee leaves the pitch with chants of *'2-1 to the referee'* ringing in his ears, although I'm not convinced about the penalty shout. Asked afterwards, Falkingham fails to make a convincing case, saying he felt contact and went down, or words to that effect.

I've spent the last twenty years listening to ex-footballers saying the same thing on Match Of The Day ad nauseam every week. *'There was contact, so he was entitled to go over,'* they appeal reasonably. *'Football's a contact sport for heaven's sake! You stay on your feet, try to get a shot away and then, only if you can't, it's a penalty!'* I scream back at the television. So there wasn't enough in our appeal for me.

It was never a free kick at the other end though.

Four defeats, and only one win in the last five home games, have propelled us out of the play off places and into ninth, as the teams immediately below us win again. The frustrating part is that four of the other teams in the top seven lost again, and we fail to take advantage.

'Sing when you're winning, you only sing when you're winning,' chanted the Town fans after the Ebbsfleet goal.

I can't help feeling that chance would be a fine thing at the moment.

Town fans wing it to watch Chesterfield kings

Chesterfield (A) W 1-0. Goal: o.g. Crowd: 4,661. Article originally published on Thursday 28th February 2019 under the title *'Winning away at Chesterfield is no mean feat for little old Town.'*

Jordan Ford is recounting the story of how he attempted to organise a coach to Barrow a few years back, having to cancel it due to lack of interest. He ended up driving over to Cumbria. The away fans numbered six.

I'm sat listening whilst sitting next to Molly on the second of two Supporters' Club coaches, organised by Jordan, heading to Chesterfield. The first, shall we say, more lively coach left two honours earlier, intent on visiting the local hostelries beforehand. Molly's struggling with her travel sickness and I'm suffering a self-inflicted hangover from the night before, so the relative peace and quiet of the second coach is welcome.

Half way down the motorway, the coach pulls up under a bridge, broken wing mirror flapping in the wind. The driver phones head office, seeking advice on whether it's safe to continue, before pulling into a nearby service station. Our trip's in jeopardy, so Jordan springs into action. On finding no tape on sale in the shop, he flashes his eyelids at the assistant behind the counter and she produces a box of tricks in which resides a roll of black gaffer tape. With the aid of a temporarily commandeered bin lid to stand on, the driver manages to shore up the broken mirror and we're on our way again, promising to call in for petrol next time. Things look up even further when Molly and I win the football card draw and pocket £20.

It's a first visit to Chesterfield for Town. The Spireites relocated in 2010 from the 138 year old historic Saltergate site to a soulless retail park, the admittedly smart new stadium fitting seamlessly alongside Tesco and Asda superstores. *'But what will you do for food?'* asked my wife, whilst filling a bag full of supermarket products before we left. Oh the glorious irony.

The big news is that Kelvin Langmead starts alongside Howe in central defence. Town are without a clean sheet since October but, with regards to the eight they kept before that, Langmead started in every one, playing alongside Howe for seven of them.

Town take the game by the scruff of the neck from the off and Kerry is unlucky not to score early on, before a trademark back-post-corner-to-Howe routine causes mayhem, leading to our hosts slicing a dangerous Thomson cross into their own net. The 230 travelling fans go wild as the Town players run over to celebrate in front of a sea of yellow and black, leaving a forlorn Chesterfield defender, head in hands, on the floor.

We have a couple of other chances to increase our lead, before Chesterfield see a fair bit of possession towards half-time, Town defending well and restricting them to a couple of hopeless long range efforts. My only concern is that we're sitting a little deep and letting them run at us at times.

The second half sees Town start to harass the Chesterfield back line higher up the pitch again, pushing for a second to kill the game off, and agonisingly putting a few decent chances past the post.

The home team eventually manage to claw their way into the game for the final fifteen minutes, with everything aimed towards their huge centre forward Denton. *'He always scores against Town,'* appears to be the consensus of opinion around me. Yet the visiting defence stands up heroically, snapping at heels, putting heads and bodies on the line.

Led by the youth element, we launch into a crazy five minute version of *'Ally Ally Ally Oh, HTFC, Yellow Black Army'*, trying to sing the players over the line. Three added minutes feel like ten. It looks like we're going to do it, but the ball drops on to Denton's head eight yards out and it's last minute at Halifax all over again. Our defenders have lost him for the one and only time… Belshaw is helpless… I can barely look as the ball arrows goalwards… before cannoning off the base of the far post and away.

It's those fine lines that can win games, and today Town have earned that little slice of luck.

The outpouring of joy at the final whistle is something to behold, as we rush to the front to celebrate the win and, yes, CLEAN SHEET with the players. We believe, they believe. It's game back on.

Little old Town have won at Chesterfield, and that's no mean achievement in my book.

The greatest cockney rip-off? Rip it up and start again

Dagenham & Redbridge (H) D 1-1. Goal: Howe. Crowd: 1,262. Bromley (H) W 1-0. Goal: Muldoon (pen). Crowd: 789. Article originally published on Thursday 7th March 2019 under the title *'Another late goal, but this time we're not on the receiving end.'*

Bromley at home on a Tuesday night may not be a major attraction for many judging by the lower than average turnout, but my daughter and I wouldn't be anywhere else. I harbour pretentions of sitting in the stand tonight, but Molly isn't having any of it. She'd enjoyed sitting in the stand at Chesterfield so much that I thought she might go for it, but she's insistent she prefers standing. That's my girl!

In direct contrast to Dagenham and Redbridge on Saturday, the first period is end-to-end. How we manage to reach half-time goalless is anyone's guess. Town in particular are unlucky, Thomson hitting the post, the Bromley keeper performing heroics and the ball just not falling kindly for our attackers in the penalty area. Although Bromley look dangerous on the break, they're a shadow of the team that would have hammered Town early on in the season if it hadn't been for Belshaw. And for that I'm grateful.

As the second half wears on, Town are still dictating the play, but the visitors have degenerated into spoiling mode, encouraged by the hapless referee. A series of bizarre indecisions sees the official wave away a stonewall penalty appeal as Beck is mugged at the back post in the fashion of Harry Kane in the World Cup, before ignoring multiple instances of the same player being wrestled to the ground. He then proceeds to compound these errors by penalising Beck if he so much as touches an opposition player. Bromley, of course, have cottoned on that if they go down when challenged by any Town player, and stay down, he's going to blow for a foul.

It's just not falling for us, as Burrell slams a shot unluckily off the crossbar and the keeper again denies Emmett. Frustration starts to set in alongside the tension, some fans calling for the manager to change things as the game appears to be edging towards a goalless draw. Harsh, I think, as the team are playing well as a unit. Even so, I'm not hopeful of the deadlock being broken, although Molly's in her usual positive mode. *'I think we're going to win it 1-0, dad,'* she says.

Eventually, Beck wins a free kick and celebrates it like a goal, as do the crowd. The referee doesn't book him for disrespect. Maybe things are starting to look up.

As we creep into the last of four added minutes, a mighty goalmouth scramble ensues as Bromley bodies block another Town attempt near the line. We scream for handball, more in hope than expectation, and the man in the middle blows and points to the spot. I almost can't bear to look as Bromley argue and Muldoon lines up to take it. Muldoon, who may well not have been on the pitch by now if the manager had chosen to make his usual substitution, a supporter standing next to me wisely points out.

Pressure? Don't you believe it. The coolest man in the ground calmly strokes the ball into the bottom corner and delirium ensues. All the pent-up frustration is released as Town players run towards us screaming in joy.

There's no time for Bromley to mount a comeback as Town close them down from the kick off. On the final whistle, an almighty scuffle breaks out amongst the players as Town celebrate and the visitors' frustration boils over. It's a very sweet win indeed, and just reward for the 789 hardy regulars.

Sometimes Karma is a wonderful thing.

Footnote: My original plan for this column after the injury time setback against Dagenham was to highlight the problem with Town not being able to finish teams off when on top, before running out of steam in the final stages as our opponents chase the game. This was also evidenced in last minute setbacks against Halifax and Ebbsfleet and it could have happened at Chesterfield, but for the width of a post. The players' superb ninety minute performance against Bromley just ripped all of that up. Football never fails to surprise.

The joy of Essex

Braintree Town (A) W 4-0. Goals: Emmett, Beck 2, Thomson. Crowd: 362. Article originally published on Thursday 14th March 2019 under the title *'Recent resurgence has left me dreaming of glory once again.'*

As I sit down to write, the big news this evening is that Wrexham are three goals down at half-time. Seven of the top nine are in action. Town aren't playing, of course, so instead I'm willing Aldershot to make a stunning second half comeback against Orient, Hartlepool to fluke an equaliser at Fylde, and Gateshead and Solihull to take points off each other.

Despite this, my daughter thinks I'm unduly pessimistic.

She bases her opinion on the fact that I frequently come out with phrases such as *'Town are dropping too deep here,'* followed by *'You could see that coming a mile off,'* when the late equaliser materialises as a result of Town dropping too deep. As evidenced in this very column last week, I also have a penchant for giving up any hope of a late winner, whilst she remains optimistic to the end.

I must protest, however, that she's got me all wrong. The instances above aren't a result of any glass-half-empty mindset, just a way of me trying to manage expectation.

It's here that I have a confession to make.

I'm not afraid to admit that I've never given up on Town achieving promotion this season. Back in August, I secretly harboured thoughts of them going straight up again, as Champions. Yes, I thought they were that good. Hopeless optimism it may turn out to be, but you couldn't call it pessimism. Of course, in public, I stated that I'd be happy with fifth from bottom come the end of the season. Managing expectation, you see.

Since hitting top spot, ten games in at Gateshead, my faith has been slowly tested with our gradual slide down the play off places.

Three wins in four, the latest a 4-0 demolition of rock bottom Braintree Town at the weekend has me dreaming once more, if a little frustrated at the fact that had we not dropped so many recent home points, we'd have been right up there near the top again. It was a truly professional performance from Town in deepest Essex, so professional in fact, that for the first time this season I completely lost interest in Barry Parker's second half commentary, such was our total domination over a shell-shocked home team. Normally, I'm glued to the radio when not able to get to the game, kicking every ball, willing us to hold on, but this game was put to bed within ten first half minutes.

So I'm now back to spending hours staring at the league table working out all possible permutations going forward for the next ten matches. In reality it's a waste of my time, as football never happens the way you want it to happen. I'd be better off ignoring what everyone else does and just concentrating on Town, one game at a time. But still I can't help myself.

'Wrexham have lost, leaving Town six points behind with two games in hand and yet to visit north Wales. Can we finish in third place..?' is the thought currently going through my head.

And if you think that's not going to happen, just bear this crazy outcome in mind from tonight's fixtures... Sutton United 0 Braintree Town 3.

On a slightly different note, the Supporters' Club are running two coaches to Barrow, a week on Saturday. One of them will be a family coach, with under-16s travelling free. It should make for a good atmosphere in Cumbria. Why not make a day of it if you haven't been away with the Supporters' Club before?

Hand in glove, the good people laugh

Maidenhead United (H) W 1-0. Goal: Beck. Crowd: 1,105. Barnet (A)
L 0-1. Crowd: 849. Article originally published on Thursday 21st
March 2019 under the title *'Barnet encounter proves to be a game too
far for Town players.'*

'Oh no, we've got a right finicky one here,' I think quietly to
myself, as Falkingham attempts to take an early free kick
quickly in midfield and the man in black forces him to take it
again as a result of a non-stationary ball. Molly wants to know
what's happening and there follows a long discussion on why
a free kick is also known as a dead ball situation. And that,
dear reader, is probably the highlight of an ordinary first half
in which, well, not much happens. There's plenty of
endeavour from both teams, but not a lot to shout about in
terms of goalmouth action, with crosses and the final pass
often going astray.

I'm mildly surprised at the larger than expected
Maidenhead turnout in the Kop and the variety of different
coloured banners, until I learn that a mini bus load of South
Shields' fans have swelled the attendance following the
postponement of their match at Workington. They must be
wishing they'd gone straight home.

In fairness to the players, it's heavy going out there today
with lashing rain and swirling wind. Standing snuggly in the

stands, you tend to forget how bad the conditions are when the 3G playing surface looks and plays like a billiard table. Two seasons ago, the pitch would have been a waterlogged mudbath and South Shields' fans may well have been making the trip elsewhere.

The second half starts in the same war of attrition vein, before two moments of high quality decide the match.

It's deja vu, as Falkingham plays a quick free kick square across the half way line and the referee pulls him back for a moving ball. The Maidenhead defence line up expecting a high second ball towards the box, but the quick thinking midfielder plays a low forward pass to Muldoon on the edge of the area. *'That's a great ball!'* I shout to Molly, as Muldoon flicks it out to Thomson who then picks out an unmarked Beck at the back post right in front of us. 1-0.

The game then reverts to type. It's nervy, and even though Town are defending well, you know the visitors are going to create at least one chance. It comes in the form of a free kick from the left and a header from no more than eight yards out. I groan inwardly as the ball heads towards the back of the distant net, before a hand stretches out and somehow diverts the ball onto the crossbar. Comparisons have been made to Gordon Banks' save against Pele in the 1970 World Cup and, while I wouldn't go that far, as Banks got a downward bullet header up and over the bar, it truly is a wonderful save from Belshaw.

The only other incident of note sees the visitors' notably grumpy right back go down in the 93rd minute complaining, whilst holding aloft a finger in his right gloved hand. Quick as a flash, a Town fan shouts *'He's broken a nail, quick bring him a new one,'* as the physio runs on. In a fit of pique, the right back throws his other glove away as the Town fans serenade him with a chorus of *'He wears his mom's gloves.'* To compound the element of farce, the ball boy carefully picks up the discarded gloves and places them back alongside the beleaguered full back. He's alright, of course, save for a shattered ego.

I hate to wish my life away, but the final whistle can't come soon enough. It's certainly not been a classic, but Town have ground out the third 1-0 win in five today. We exit the ground happy, wishing the South Shields' contingent a safe journey home, four points clear of Gateshead in eighth with two games in hand.

A Tuesday night trip to north London sees us with the chance of going fourth with a win. I'd originally wanted to go, but in the clash between the need to be present to supervise a construction site, versus the need to take two days off to watch a football match, common sense kicked in. It was brilliant though to see 90 Town fans there out of a crowd of 943, swelled by a thirty strong southern contingent.

It turns out to be a game too far for a group of players who'd put in such a shift, with no substitutions, at the weekend. Simon Weaver spoke of a lack of intensity, and a timidness in the first thirty minutes that lost us the game. In reality, Barnet did to us what we've been doing to our opponents in the last few games, taking a one goal lead and holding it. Even so, you could sense the nervousness around the ground as Town pressed hard for an equaliser in the closing stages, Belshaw playing as an outfield player and coming oh so close at the death. What a story that would have been!

But it wasn't to be.

Here we are nowhere

Barrow AFC (A) D 2-2. Goals: Muldoon, Howe. Crowd:1,934. Article originally published on Thursday 28th March 2019 under the title *'My trip to Barrow – a tough place to come in more ways than one.'*

Don't laugh but, growing up as a child, I had a fascination with 'exotic', far-flung places such as Barrow, Workington and... Stranraer. They were names familiar to me from the football results on a Saturday and my collection of programmes from every club in the English and Scottish leagues. Barrow and Workington in particular were all the more fascinating because they were both clubs that had tumbled out of the Football League, a feat that was hard to achieve in those pre-automatic promotion and relegation days. Barrow failed in their bid to seek re-election in 1972, being replaced by Hereford United.

I've never lost this fascination, so today's a rare treat for me, as it's my first ever visit to Barrow-in-Furness during the hours of daylight. The cynics amongst you may say it's better seen in the dark, but I'm going to put my fingers in my ears and ignore you.

Once we get to the Lakes, it seems to take forever to reach Barrow itself, lying as it does in isolated detachment at the bottom of a long peninsula, overlooking the Irish Sea. There's only one road in; it's often described as the *'longest cul de sac in* Britain,' so it's not somewhere you go unless you have to. It's certainly not somewhere I can take the family for a day out when visiting the Lakes. Much as I want to. In 2014, the Office For National Statistics judged Barrow to be the most miserable town in Britain.

We're on the family coach and arrive at the ground on the insalubrious edge of town an hour early. I have to curtail an urge to walk further into the town centre, as I don't think Molly will share my fascination with gritty, northern industrial towns. We adjourn to The Soccer Bar on the main road instead and sit down with a few of the regulars, none of whom speak to us incomers from another planet. I wait for the rest of the Town fans to come in and liven up proceedings, but it turns out they've all gone to the social club next to the ground. Molly wants to know why it's called the Soccer Bar when we're in England.

Holker Street has been Barrow's home since 1909, and it's an old fashioned, no thrills football ground, on three sides at least. Town fans are segregated on an open terrace, behind and to the side of one goal. The old roof has long been lost to health and safety concerns and a lone, windswept snack van stands in the back corner. It really could be a scene from the 1970s.

The opposite Steelworks End of the ground was demolished in the early seventies in order to accommodate a speedway track. It was that decision to host speedway that partly did for Barrow's league status, along with its geographic isolation, and Hereford's famous FA Cup win over Newcastle. The speedway team, Barrow Bombers, lasted three seasons at Holker Street before being turfed out. The terrace was never rebuilt and the aforementioned social club stands there now.

The Cumbrians were supported by a colourful band of supporters called Ultras Barrovia as recently as 2012 but, unusually, there's no home choir, and not one banner or flag in evidence today, even though there's a good home turnout approaching 2,000. It's left to us to make what noise we can in the open end.

The Town players can't cope with the home side first half, struggling to string more than two passes together as a very good Barrow team win the midfield battle, and attack us at pace all over the pitch. Tempers fray. Howe is spoken to by the referee for arguing with Belshaw, whilst Falkingham riles the nearby home terrace by going down to a tackle from behind like he's been shot. Twice. We're lucky to go in only two down and it doesn't bode well for the second half. I'm beginning to question my sanity.

Having left all our chocolate on the coach, Molly and I queue at the snack van, emerging five minutes later with a solitary Twix between us. You have to take your pleasure where you can. We're just in the process of savouring it, only half paying attention, barely two minutes into the second half, when Muldoon chases down a lost cause and the ball ricochets off his chest towards the goal. Stood, as we are, side on, in front of the snack van, we're not sure whether it's heading in. The net ripples and we belatedly fling our arms in the air.

Barrow then charge down the other end and Belshaw's goal leads a charmed life as his defenders clear two goal bound efforts from near the line, but Town are gradually clawing their way back into the game. Half-time substitute Leesley plants a swirling, trademark corner onto Howe's head and we're unbelievably back level. Cue unbridled joy in the Town end. We run down to the players to celebrate.

And that's how it stays. Barrow's a tough place to come in more ways than one and it's a great point, dug out by a group of players who don't know when to give up.

We travel home happy, leaving Barrovians a little more miserable, although I'd personally have liked to have seen a bit more of downtown Barrow-in-Furness. Maybe next time and, while I'm on the subject, maybe we'll draw Workington away in the FA Cup next season.

Stranraer, on the other hand, may prove to be a little more difficult. How about a pre-season trip to Scotland, Town?

'Displaying common sense like that, are you sure she's really your daughter?'

Salford City (H) L 0-1. Crowd: 1,700. Maidstone United (H) D 2-2. Goals: Beck, Muldoon (pen). Crowd: 1,134. Article originally published on Thursday 4th April 2019 under the title *'It hasn't been the best week, but we're still in a really good position.'*

I think it's safe to say that it hasn't been the best week for Town.

Sadly, against Salford, there was to be no repeat of our previous glorious performance in front of the BT Sport cameras. We had the better of a tight first period and could have gone in ahead with more composure in front of goal, but Salford made the most of a dangerous spell just after half-time, despite Belshaw's best efforts, and were then happy to sit back as their three huge centre backs mopped up high balls with ease. They looked well organised and the Town players never got near to the dangerous attacking football displayed in such abundance in Greater Manchester earlier in the season.

The turning point of the match against Maidstone the following Saturday was a tight offside decision that went against us just before half-time. Obsessively pausing the match highlights over and over, Beck looked level to me, and 2-0 before half-time would have killed the visitors off. Unfortunately they then went down the other end, with the

[105]

wonderfully, if inaccurately, named Amaluzor picking up a loose pass and unleashing a swerving screamer past Belshaw. He then proceeded to repeat the feat early in the second half. The visiting fans must have been a tad shocked, seeing as the aforementioned Amaluzor had only scored three goals in twenty seven matches prior to kick off. Sometimes you just can't legislate for things like that.

Town had the bulk of possession, but the trademark quick-fire passing game that stretches opponents defensively, was only seen for fifteen minutes after the second Maidstone goal, and the game eventually petered out into a frustrating draw. It was two points dropped that would have put us five points clear of eighth place with five games to go.

With Braintree winning, Maidstone went bottom, yet their fans and players celebrated like they'd won the Champions League. I pointed this out to Molly. *'It's what we did at Barrow,'* she wisely retorted.

An unscientific survey of Town-supporting Stray* dog walkers and other Town home regulars confirms a few things I've been thinking for a while.

There's a recognition that the pacey, attacking pass and move football of the first half of the season, although still there in fits and starts, has been in shorter supply recently. The long spell without a clean sheet has led to a slightly more cautious approach, with the ball going backwards and sideways more often. Maidstone's first corner on Saturday, a few minutes in, saw every Town player back defending it.

Opponents pressing high up the pitch, to nullify our passing out from the back, has led to the employment of more long balls. I'm all in favour of mixing it up and keeping your opponents guessing, especially if they're giving you no time to pass and move, but our long balls are too often hopeful punts to the head of an isolated Beck, rather than incisive longer balls to a dangerous runner. The long ball routine straight from kick off, as a statement of intent, just isn't working.

The overall impression though, despite the recent setbacks, is that we'd have taken the position we're in now at the start of the season, and there's a recognition that we can't be world beaters every week in our first ever spell in such a tough league. Although we'd certainly take promotion, a period of consolidation isn't a bad thing. This is little Harrogate Town, rubbing shoulders with Wrexham, Orient, Hartlepool, Chesterfield, and sitting in a league above York and Stockport. A team from a previously largely non-footballing town that was attracting crowds of barely 250 only a short while ago. Just pause and think on that.

Trudging back through the ginnel on the way home after the Salford defeat, I'm fretting about whether we'll make the play offs with visits to Wrexham and Orient to come. *'Chill dad,'* says a Zen-like Molly, *'we'll either get promoted to the league above, which will be fantastic, or we'll stay in the league we're in which is also fantastic.'* No taking to the internet to criticise the manager or disappointment with the players, she's happy to accept things for what they are. And to think I used to worry that she'd lose interest if and when Town started losing.

I repeated this story to the boss at work. His response was cutting. *'Displaying common sense like that, are you sure she's really your daughter?'*

*See footnote on page 149.

You can't moan can you?

Havant & Waterlooville (A) W 2-1. Goals: Woods, Thomson. Crowd: 937. Article originally published on Thursday 11th April 2019 under the title *'Weaver gets his tactics just right as Town consolidate play-off spot.'*

Whilst trudging home through the ginnel with my daughter following the Salford defeat two weeks ago, I found myself fretting about whether we'd make the play offs with visits to Wrexham And Orient yet to come.

'Chill dad,' said a Zen-like Molly, *'we'll either get promoted to the Football League, which will be fantastic, or we'll stay in the league we're in, which is also fantastic.'* *

This week I find myself in the record shop in town, just as one of the guys behind the counter informs me that Town are one down at Havant and Waterlooville.

Leaving the shop, slightly despondent, new purchases in hand, I decide to take Molly's advice to *'chill'*. What will be will be. The play-offs are over-rated anyway.

I check my phone opposite Betty's, more in hope than expectation, and my eyes land on *'GOAL. Muldoon 42.'* I blink, and blink again. It's still there. Rushing back to the car to tune into Radio York, I find out my phone has lied. It was Woods who beat Muldoon in the race to tap in from two yards following a Hawks defensive howler. Come on Town!

As the second half wears on, a draw's no good for either side. The winning goal, when it eventually comes nine minutes from time, is a result of a quick-thinking long ball from Kitching down the left wing. Muldoon's darting run and cross being converted via the unlikely source of Thomson's head. It's a great goal: incisive, direct and well-worked.

Joy leads to farce in the Town end as the away supporters rush to the front to celebrate with the players and an unlocked perimeter gate swings open, depositing several fans onto the floor in front of the players, collapsing one by one like a deck of cards. It's one almighty pile-on. The players look on in bemusement before being summoned back on to the pitch by the referee's whistle. Agnew stoops to help a fan up, Muldoon just stands and laughs. I look forward to seeing the video replayed on *'You've Been Framed'.*

Simon Weaver's tactics today have been spot on, addressing the tentative, hit and hope play we've seen creep in during recent games and replacing it with penetrative football on the ground, runners down the flanks and Woods in a roaming number ten role. When you stretch an opposing defence like this, you can then play the surprise long ball and get in behind.

The result virtually condemns the home team to relegation along with fellow newcomers from the National League South, Braintree. Meanwhile Salford, Fylde, Solihull Moors and ourselves, all newcomers from the stronger National League North, are in the top six. The magnitude of Town's achievement these past two seasons in getting out of such a tough league and competing at the higher level is not to be underestimated.

The home commentator, sharing commentary duties with Barry Parker today, is quite taken with our possession football and states that we *'look a very impressive side going into the play-offs.'* Let's hope he's right, as this vital win takes us five points clear of Ebbsfleet in eighth, with four games to play. It really is the hope I can't stand.

*Yes, I know I wrote that at the end of the previous week's column, but the Advertiser chose to edit out my final punch line and end it at 'Just pause and think on that'. I wouldn't normally mind, as I'm sure it was due to space restrictions or the fact that 'Just pause and think on that,' is a good way to end a column, however I'd read the end of my planned column to the aforementioned boss at work, and he was looking forward to seeing his words of wisdom printed in the newspaper.

I just can't
be happy today

Boreham Wood (H) L 0-1. Crowd: 1,216. Article originally published on Thursday 18th April 2019 under the title *'A frustratingly flat performance as we approach squeaky bum time.'*

As we've witnessed Town battling with the big boys in their maiden National League season, I hope these columns have managed to reflect the excitement, enthusiasm and humour, displayed both on and off the pitch. I would be the first to admit, however, that the frustratingly flat performance against Boreham Wood this week has made this latest instalment very difficult to write.

If you were a visitor from out of space, just happening to land at Wetherby Road, thirty minutes into the game on Saturday, you'd have been forgiven for thinking that the team needing three points to help cement a play-off place were the team in the flashy sky blue and black strip.

Pre-kick off, Luke Garrard, the larger than life visiting manager strode across the pitch like a film star to embrace Simon Weaver, before his players, all seemingly six foot plus giants that work out daily, proceeded to boss the Town players on the pitch. Boreham Wood got the early goal through a well-worked corner routine, and the expected Town reaction never came, as the visitors pushed us back to the edge of our own area. Falkingham was given no time on the ball and, without Emmett orchestrating from midfield, we lacked bravery going forward. There was a long period where

Town couldn't get even hold of the ball, let alone get out of their own half, as the visitors won nearly every fifty-fifty challenge and sprayed the ball around with aplomb. Their precarious position near the bottom four was a mystery to most of us watching.

Town rallied slightly before half-time, Howe coming close despite being held in the area, and we hoped for a better second half attacking towards the Kop as the visitors tired. Although there was an improvement on the first half, it never really happened and, when Town did threaten sporadically, the Boreham Wood keeper was equal to everything. The visitors turned holding in the area into an art form and the referee was the latest in a long, undistinguished line of officials that seem to think it's part of the rules of the game. It felt like we could have continued playing until midnight without scoring.

It was nice to see Jordan Thewlis back following his long lay-off. His pace will be a good option to have going into the final few games. I was convinced he was going to see red though, as his frustration with being held in the area led to him landing a fairly weak punch on their goal scorer, Champion. The referee ran across to consult with the linesman and, after what seemed like an age, the card was yellow. At least he was consistently useless.

Five minutes were added on at the end, but not even Molly's usual positivity could summon a grand finale, the visitors missing a one-on-one and hitting the bar from three yards out in the final minutes.

To compound my misery, I felt a chill all second half, blaming it on the wind blowing through the new exits cut into the back of the Kop in order to increase the capacity. When I got home, I realised I'd forgotten to put my jumper on.

The only real positive to come out of the whole afternoon was that Ebbsfleet also lost badly at home. It's nice to know they're feeling the same pressure as we are.

It's squeaky bum time heading into the last three matches, but incredibly exciting with our match at Leyton Orient on Good Friday now on BT Sport (we're becoming regulars!) and the prospect of two of the new stands opening for the final home match against Gateshead on Easter Monday. We're going to have to try them both out.

Here's hoping that next week finds me in a happier mood, with Emmett back fit and Town having secured a play-off place.

It's the Harrogate girls making all the noise, as Town secure play-offs

Leyton Orient (A) L 0-2. Crowd: 6.665. Gateshead (H) W 2-0. Goals: Thewlis, Beck. Crowd: 1,629. Wrexham (A) L 1-2. Goal: Beck. Crowd: 3,690. Article originally published on Thursday 25th April 2019 under the title *'Anything from here is a bonus, but who knows just how far we can go.'*

'We're the yellow black army...' is the chant echoing from our front garden.

My daughter's teaching four of her friends Town songs in readiness for the showdown with Gateshead. They're coming with her to Town for the first time on Easter Monday, after they've all been into Harrogate shopping. They've set up a chat group called 'town and Town'.

I head out for Domino's pizza, as the strains of *'Simon Weaver's Barmy Army...'* follows me down the street. Everywhere we go, it's the Harrogate girls making all the noise, I think to myself.

Gateshead's win over Chesterfield on Good Friday, coupled with our brave defeat at Leyton Orient, in front of the biggest crowd ever to witness a Town team, puts the visitors back in with a shout of stealing a play off place if they can win today. Town need three points to get safely over the line.

It's the final home match in bright sunshine, and it feels like the play off semi-final against Chorley last year all over again in terms of both importance and excitement. We may not go on to win the play-offs, but we sure as hell want to get there.

With the Wetherby Road stand given over to the travelling Gateshead fans, ousted home fans populate the big new terrace next to the Johnstone's Paint Stand in one great splash of colour. Myself and five teenagers, their cheeks bedecked with yellow and black stripes, try out the new 1919 end stand for size, as do the Town choir. The addition of the new stands gives the ground a proper football league atmosphere.

The players start nervously, struggling to put two passes together, as Gateshead push us back. They're giving us no space or time to play out from the back, snapping into the tackles and spraying the ball around as Town struggle to get out of their own half. You can feel the tension in the crowd, as the 1919 end falls quiet. It's last week's horror show against Boreham Wood all over again, but with two notable exceptions: the visitors aren't all over six feet tall and Town hold firm with few scares at the back.

It's forty one minutes in and we've barely had a sniff going forward. The ball's been mostly down the other end and Molly's friends must be wondering what all the fuss is about. Then Falkingham plays a slide rule through ball and Thewlis is in. It looks like the keeper might get there first, but Jordan nicks it, runs round him, takes one look up, and slides the ball into the empty net ahead of the retreating defenders. Yes! Having hit the post and had one cleared off the line in similar circumstances in west London three days ago, this is an advert for keeping your nerve.

Town come out all guns blazing in the second half, doing to Gateshead what they did to us in the first half. The Kop takes up the challenge and roars the team on.

Ten minutes in, Thewlis hurdles over a tackle brilliantly on the touch line and he's away again, flying into the area before sliding the ball across the six yard box on a plate for the arriving Beck. We erupt with joy as the ball hits the net in front of us. Molly runs across in excitement to tell me that Ebbsfleet are one down to Dover. We might just actually do it.

The Town fans serenade the travelling fans with a song about how they're only here because Sunderland are, well, to put it politely, rubbish. Someone needs to tell them Gateshead's next to Newcastle. Or maybe that's the subtle point of the song, call the visitors part-timers and Mackems at the same time and, hey presto, two 'insults' in one. Hopefully they took it in the humour it was intended.

Back on the pitch, the visitors are on the ropes as Town mount wave after wave of attacks, utilising the width of the playing surface and having two 'goals' chalked off for offside in the process, before seeing the final twenty minutes out with only the one minor scare, as Burrell tries to head over his own keeper in sympathy. Belshaw, as always, is alert to the occasion. Thewlis is substituted to a deserved standing ovation to be replaced by... George Thomson. With Muldoon and a fit again Knowles also sitting on the bench, our attacking options look good going forward into the play-offs.

We exit the ground happy, having given the players a rousing send off in the final home match of the season. Making the top seven in our maiden National League campaign is a brilliant achievement.

There's been some speculation amongst Town fans as to whether Fylde or Wrexham are the best opponents in the play-offs. Personally, I don't care. I'd prefer to travel to Fylde, but Wrexham are in a bit of a sticky patch form-wise. Either way, we've got to overturn a run of results that has seen us gain only two wins against top seven teams, both of these at Wetherby Road. Can we break through that glass ceiling I alluded to earlier in the season? It's a tall order and the form book over the season says no, but we go into the play-offs as underdogs with absolutely nothing to lose. Anything from here on in is a bonus and, if we believe in ourselves, who knows where it can take us.

Luddite: 'a mantle worn with rebellious pride'

Article originally published on Thursday 2nd May 2019 under the title *'Sometimes, being a bit of a Luddite actually has distinct advantages.'*

'It's pretty simple. You just do it through your bank,' says Jordan Ford, the coach organiser, as he talks me though how to pay online for mine and Molly's coach tickets to Fylde. I normally prefer to pay in cash on the coach, but Jordan's trying to move away from that as he usually ends up with large amounts of cash burning a hole in his pocket at the match. The thing is, it might seem simple to Jordan, but I'm a bit of a Luddite with that type of thing, so I arrange to drop the money off in an envelope at his house instead. On hearing this, my wife rolls her eyes and sorts it all out online in five minutes.

The punishing, short timetable for teams in the play-off quarter final matches means that I'm having to write this column on the eve of the Wednesday Fylde showdown, in order to hit deadline day for a newspaper that comes out on the Thursday after the match. So by the time you sit down to read this, Town may be already on the eve of a historic National League play-off semi final at Solihull. Or not, as the case may be. To further confuse matters, by the time I come to write next week's column, Town could be on the way to

Wembley. Or our season could again be over. To that end, I think it's futile to make any kind of prediction as I'll only be hopelessly out-of-date.

If you find all of that a little confusing, just spare a thought for us Town fans seeking to travel over to Fylde to attend the match. Let me try to explain...

Fylde initially reduced ticket prices for the tie as a *'thank you'* to their fans and in order to encourage more neutrals through the gate. All good so far, you may think, and up until Tuesday, around ninety Town fans had purchased tickets online for the away end at these cheaper prices.

Then, totally out of the blue, as I was sitting down to pen this column, a minor spat broke out between the clubs. Fylde issued a statement on Tuesday evening, only twenty four hours before the match, to the effect that they had just been informed by Town that ticket price reductions for a play-off match were against National League rules and that this had been confirmed by the National League itself. Town, for their part, stated that they had pointed this out on the Sunday they went on sale.

It seems that, as the visiting team is entitled to half of the gate receipts, Town weren't happy at not being consulted. Fylde then stated they were willing to make up the difference for their home fans, but not for visiting fans. So Town fans were asked to repurchase tickets at the increased price, whilst home fans maintained their reduced-price tickets.

To further rub salt into the wounds, it wasn't clear when refunds would be forthcoming, so visiting fans were forced to buy new tickets *before* receiving a refund for the old, cancelled ones. This led, as you may imagine to utter confusion, with some Town fans having paid for two tickets upfront at different prices, some saying they would turn up with the old tickets, hoping they would be honoured, whilst others not online at the time would presumably be totally unaware of the change.

To pile more chaos onto the confusion, Fylde advertised the new price of £5 for U16 standing on their ticketing site and then took £10 off people in the payment process, leading to the ludicrous situation of U16s being sold incorrect tickets *twice*. And this was all after their website had originally stated that away tickets were sold out on Tuesday afternoon, again incorrectly.

The ultimate irony of this farce, which makes the Brexit negotiations seem almost sane in comparison, is that in attempting to deal with a breach of League rules in this uneven manner, Fylde have seemingly broken another rule. You can't charge away fans more than home fans for comparable tickets. Let's just hope that the home team's defence is as disorganised as their ticketing office.

They would of course be hearing from my solicitor, if it wasn't for the fact that I don't have one and, as I haven't actually gotten round to buying tickets yet, I've successfully avoided all the heartache. My preference is to amble up to the ground and buy them on the gate in the good old fashioned way. And, with Fylde seeking to charge my daughter a tenner online, there's no chance of me doing anything else now. We can even choose to pay less and go in the home end if we desire, although I think that may be a step too far in order to save £6.

Sometimes, being a bit of a luddite has its distinct advantages.

The dream is over.
For this season
at least

AFC Fylde (A) L 1-3 (Play-Off Quarter Final). Goal: o.g.. Crowd: 1,560. Article originally published on Thursday 9th May 2019 under the title 'A National League Play-Off Spot? You bet we'd have taken that at the start.'

Having read my column last week regarding the Fylde pricing fiasco, with Town fans forced to buy tickets online twice and me confessing that I preferred to pay on the gate in order to avoid all the hassle, Molly's concerned.

'I wish you'd bought tickets in advance Dad,' she says, 'what happens if we can't get in?'

I try to reassure her that the match isn't all-ticket and that there's a sizeable away end. 'We'll be fine,' I say, rather unconvincingly.

She need not have worried. On boarding the coach, we find out that half the occupants of the back seats have spare tickets of course, although they're all offering us the more expensive ones! 'No thanks, we'll pay when we get there,' I retort. That way, if the coach breaks down, I've not lost my admission fee.

Arriving safely in Lancashire, the good news is that sanity's been restored and cheaper admission prices are available for all fans. Mill Farm is a modern, new build stadium in a sports complex on the main road between

Preston and Blackpool adjacent to an Aldi, a KFC... and not much else. It's slightly strange because they've only built stands on three sides of the ground, although there looks to be room to build a fourth. With only 1,560 in for such an important play-off match, it appears there's no need to build behind the far goal just yet though.

'Ten pounds in and there's no one here...' sing the Town fans.

It's a sizeable Town turnout of around 250 for an early 7pm kick off that's being televised. We have the entire 1,000 capacity covered terrace behind one goal (told you so, Molly) and the players are greeted with a barrage of yellow and black ticker tape and balloons.

Although the home side have plenty of possession early doors, the first chances go to Town, in front of the travelling fans, with the Fylde keeper pulling off two sharp saves. The referee's forced to stop the game twice whilst Fylde players burst pitch-invading balloons to a chorus of boos from the away end. We're doing our best to sing the ball into the net, but depressingly find ourselves two down inside a crazy five minutes. It looks like a long way back and Town are defending dangerously too deep at times, struggling to keep possession when they do have it. We look decidedly second best.

'Two nil and you still don't sing...'

But if there's been one defining theme about the team this season, it's that they never know when they're beaten. Somehow, Town manage to claw their way into the game approaching half-time. Thewlis skips past the keeper, who hauls him down. Penalty! We chant for the keeper's dismissal. The referee doesn't even flash yellow. There's nervous excitement in the Town end as Muldoon runs up in front of us. He puts it low to the same side as the last gasp winner at home to Bromley, but the keeper's done his homework and gets a hand to it. It's agony.

The second half sees Town come out determined to have a go. Joe Leesley's on, pinging dangerous crosses into the Fylde box. Ten minutes in, a trademark Leesley free kick causes chaos and a Fylde defender puts into his own net. There's a delayed reaction as it's hard to see what's happened from the Town end. Then jubilant Town players wheel away, arms aloft in celebration, and the away end erupts. Is the fight back underway? Can we do a Barrow?

Now it's Fylde's turn to struggle to get out of their own half as Town press high, flinging crosses into the distant area.

'Na na na-na na na na, yellow black army...'

The Town fans haven't stopped singing all night, even when two down, and we sure as hell aren't going to stop now. There are a few near misses and goalmouth scrambles but, frustratingly, nothing falls decisively to a yellow and black shirt.

As caution's thrown to the wind and Howe is dispatched up front, Fylde start to pick us off on the break. Belshaw, Burrell and the right hand post play heroics in keeping them out, but a third goal in the ninetieth minute finally kills Town hopes off. Even then, there's time for another Town attempt before the referee's whistle ends the contest. Exhausted visiting players fall to the ground. The Town fans are still singing.

'Take me home Wetherby Road, to the place I belong...'

As the despondent players come over to applaud the raucous away support, and we applaud them back, Fylde celebrate. Maybe they're going to need that fourth stand after all. Our season's over in a cruel way, but we can't stay too downhearted for long. It's been one hell of an adventure and the players have done us proud. A sixth place finish in the National League and a play-off place? You bet we'd have taken that at the start of the season.

Yet the table doesn't lie. We've been good, but one victory in thirteen league and cup matches against the top five tells its own story. Next season, if we want to challenge, we need to learn to be more clinical in both boxes against the top teams, just like Fylde were tonight. And that feels a strange statement to make about a team that's proudly finished as top scorers in the National League.

Challenge? What must I be thinking? My cautious self will take consolation in our difficult second season in the National League, but my dreamer self has little old Town challenging for the Football League two seasons in a row. We can't surely. Can we?

Chapter Three
Practice makes perfect

*A second season in the National League
2019/20*

That's entertainment b/w down in the service station at midnight

Solihull Moors (H) D 2-2. Goals: Leesley, Beck. Crowd: 1,045. Barrow AFC (A) W 3-0. Goals: W. Smith 2, Hall. Crowd: 1,602. Article originally published on Thursday 8th August 2019 under the title *'Attendance aside, what a good start!'*

It's a new season and I'm admittedly more nervous than excited. It's the toughest opening day fixture we could have imagined, against last season's runners up. We're no longer the early season National League surprise package and have last season's sixth place finish to live up to. To compound matters, the visitors stole Callum Howe a week before kick-off and he lines up against us on the right side of their defence. Please don't let him score the winner.

'Where shall we stand?' asks Molly. It's a good question and one I struggle to answer. We've always traditionally stood towards the tea bar end of the Wetherby Road stand pre-kick off but now, with this having been given over to away fans, I'm feeling a tad displaced. I can see the need for segregation when Notts County and Stockport arrive in town, but Solihull Moors? Really?

We eventually settle on the Kop and then have to trudge round the ground because Town choose to attack the 1919 end. My early season nerves seem to have translated to the Town players as the visitors dictate play, twice through one-on-one, twice denied by Belshaw, before McCallum skies a soft penalty over the bar. *'What a waste of money,'* chant the Town fans, but we're only putting off the inevitable, as Moors bury a header from a corner. Town can barely muster a chance as the five man visiting midfield snuffs out our midfield and we resort to hit and hope. It's not been the best of starts, but at least it's only one at half-time.

The game turns on its head in three crazy second half minutes. Town find their feet and start playing to their strengths, keeping the ball down, spreading play to the wings and getting in behind the midfield five. A lightning break, one of many from Kiernan, wins a corner and there's in-form Leesley, placing a deep ball onto Beck's towering head. Anything Solihull can do...

The visitors are rattled, a weak defensive header falls to the feet of Leesley fully thirty yards out. *'Shoot!'* Molly and I scream in unison. Joe shifts it onto his left and does just that. The ball arcs towards us and the top corner. The keeper sees it and moves, left arm out-stretched, but the curl on the strike defeats him and the net bulges in front of us. The Kop reacts with disbelief and mayhem in equal measures. A chant of *'Callum, Callum, what's the score?'* breaks out. Personally I don't join in, not out of sympathy, but because I don't like to tempt fate.

Although we don't manage to hold on to the lead and then go on to miss a penalty of our own, fate duly tempted, I'm happy with the point. It's a long season ahead and Solihull will definitely be up there. The attitude Town show to come back into this game and boss the second half will stand them in good stead. A point's about fair for both sides.

And, looking further on the bright side, Howe didn't come back to haunt us with one of his trademark late headers. I pass him later on as he's leaving the ground to board the coach back to the Midlands. I think of setting the dog onto his ankles, but she'd probably only lick him to death. Besides, I bear him no ill wishes, apart from wanting him to regret his decision at the end of the season as Moors finish below Town.

The one concern from such a great opening match is the attendance figure of 1,045, although it felt like more, as both mine and Molly's predictions were way over. It's fully 333 down on the opening day crowd against Sutton last year and 135 down on the previous Solihull home game, which was also played in the summer holidays. I know this, because I was in the Mediterranean at the time. It's been a bit of a rough summer with the fallout over ticket prices, and the fear is that, faced with increases of £4 on both the cheapest full price adult ticket and £3 on the cheapest U16 ticket, more casual supporters, especially those with younger children, are not going to attend as often. We'll never know what the attendance would have been with a cheaper pricing structure, and we'll see how the season's average works out, but I'll end with a little cautionary tale. Bear with me.

I know someone who decided to visit Town for a match five seasons ago. He took his daughter along solely because it was only a pound in for her at the time. His daughter got hooked and they've barely missed a home match since. She's now a season ticket holder, looking forward to the trip to Barrow on Tuesday night, wants to go to more away matches and won't talk to her dad again if he doesn't let her go to Wrexham this season. They buy food, drink and merchandise at the ground and talk about Town at work and school, spreading the word amongst friends, some of whom have come to matches.

Her dad wrote an article about their adventures following Town and sent it into the *Advertiser*, who subsequently printed it and asked him to pen the very column you're reading now.

To cut a long story short, it's fair to say that if the admission prices for children had been the equivalent of today's £8 back then, Molly wouldn't be a Town fan and this column wouldn't exist.

Footnote from Barrow

9.55pm Tuesday night. We're on the coach back from deepest Cumbria and I'm happily braving travel sickness on the dark, winding road to pen this. Three goals, all scored by our new central defensive pair, a well-earned clean sheet and three valuable points from a difficult place to visit. Town fans have a new goal scoring hero in the form of Will Smith and a new song along the lines of him costing less than Callum Howe and scoring more goals.

Callum Who?

Footnote To The Footnote From Barrow

12.45am Wednesday morning. We're stuck behind an accident on a rainy M6 outside Preston. We've been here nearly two hours now, with the motorway due to re-open at 1pm. It's still another two hours home after that. Gallows humour is beginning to set in on the coach. The aroma of coach toilet is wafting down the aisle. I vaguely remember winning 3-0 at Barrow sometime yesterday in the dim distant past. I may be late into work tomorrow, sorry, today.

Molly's in for a late night also. I wonder if she still wants to go to Wrexham...

Notts County fail to deter my daughter. My job here is done

Woking (A) L 0-1. Crowd: 1,470. Notts County (H) L 0-2. Crowd: 1,863. Article originally published on Thursday 15th August 2019 under the title *'Issues need addressing quickly if we want to avoid a difficult season.'*

I've been looking forward to Town entertaining Notts County, the oldest professional club in England and one of the twelve founder members of the Football League, ever since the fixtures were announced. I'd never have dreamt of this fixture outside of the FA Cup First Round five years ago, and I certainly don't intend to take it for granted now.

Notts County were actually in the old First Division as recently as 1992, the last time Leeds won it and the year before it became the Premiership. Yes, I know it's hard to believe now, but Leeds were actually in the top tier at one time. However, I digress.

If we're going to be playing Notts County, now appears to be the best time. They've not won so far, looked poor at the weekend when losing at home to Barnet and only managed to assemble a squad two weeks before the start of the season. Let's hit them while they're looking fragile.

Unfortunately, things don't get off to a good start. And that's just off the pitch. I've left my season ticket in my wallet at work and have to sheepishly ask the office staff to let me in.

To their credit, I'm waved though with a smile, albeit feeling decidedly embarrassed.

Things don't get any better on the pitch. For the third home game running, if you count Gateshead at the end of last season, Town fail to come out of the starting blocks first half and have Belshaw to thank for keeping the score below four. The out-of-form visitors suddenly look like world-beaters, whilst Town again resort to hit and hope, struggling to put two passes together. Yet somehow, we manage to ride the storm and should be ahead towards half-time when Kiernan is denied at point blank range by the visiting keeper. It's then that the game turns on a sixpence in five disastrous first half minutes.

First, Beck is blatantly hauled down for the umpteenth time in the box and we go through the motions of appealing for a penalty. Shock sets in as the referee actually points to the spot this time. Town, having missed four penalties in a row, have passed the poisoned chalice on to Leesley. Being our dead ball specialist, I've always felt he should be our main penalty taker. He takes aim, fires... and nearly knocks out a fan to the left of the goal. What do I know? The penalty curse strikes again. *'We're Harrogate Town, we can't score a pen,'* chants the Kop. I'm considering never appealing for a foul in the box ever again, it's all too much to bear.

The visitors then go down the other end and force Town to clear off the line right before half-time. Unfortunately, it was via Will Smith's hand according to the referee and we're down to ten men. To add insult to injury, County turn out to be half-decent at taking penalties.

I'm in a deep depression at half-time and find myself apologising for Town's performance to Molly's friend, Lily, who's come to the match with us. I also find myself almost wishing the office staff hadn't let me in. I can't see any way back, but you never know.

As it turns out, ten man Town make a fairly good fist of it second half, displaying all the urgency and confidence they lacked in the first half, moving the ball with attacking intent and creativity through midfield, now Emmett's on. The visitors are rendered virtually non-existent as an attacking threat, as Weaver opts for a brave three at the back and the players try to take the game to County.

Muldoon should score when put through but his chip over the keeper is cleared off the line. It's a frustrating repeat of the defeat at Woking however, as Town could still be playing now as I write this at 12.30am, and still not have the ball in the net. The visitors eventually make their superior numbers pay and score again with their only shot on target in the second period. We applaud the players off, as they've given it their all in the second half, but that calamitous first half left them facing a mountain too far to climb.

If we are to avoid a difficult season, Town have to address a number of issues quickly. The recent failure to turn up in the first half of home matches is costing us dearly, and heaven knows where we would be in the table without Belshaw. When we do start dictating play and creating chances, we need to be more ruthless in putting those chances away. I can't even bring myself to mention penalties.

We walk home and Molly's asking about the next away matches and whether we can go. I tell her Dagenham's too far too soon, but we may be able to go to Fylde.

'When I'm sixteen and old enough to go on the coach myself, I'm going to go to all the Town matches,' Molly announces defiantly.

'What? Even if they play as badly as in the first half today?' I enquire.

'Yes,' she retorts.

I guess she's in it for life; our five hour nightmare of a coach journey back from Barrow the week before didn't put her off, and my job here is done.

You get what you deserve

Dagenham & Redbridge (A) L 2-4. Goals: o.g., Kiernan. Crowd: 1,043. Article originally published on Thursday 22nd August 2019 under the title 'Is it time to re-assess in the wake of our genuinely worrying start?'

Whilst the optimists amongst us could justifiably claim that the Woking defeat was just 'one of those days' and that Town could easily have gone on to beat Notts County if only Leesley had converted from twelve yards, the 4-2 loss to Dagenham & Redbridge offered no such solace. Even the most glass-half-full supporter would struggle to file the third defeat in eight days under the heading of 'bad luck'.

It had all started so well, with Town taking the lead twice in an exhilarating end-to-end opening twenty five minutes. Certainly there was no slow start here, but the warning signs were present in the way that the home side consistently breached the Town defence. In four of our five matches this season, we've looked incredibly open at times through the middle, with Belshaw single-handedly keeping us in the game on multiple occasions. With Callum Howe lost to Solihull, Will Smith out suspended, Lloyd Kerry injured and Liam Agnew and Toby Lees out on loan, the small squad looks wafer-thin in both defence and central midfield. The other loss less talked about is the sale of Kelvin Langmead to Brackley. How we could dearly do with someone of his experience in our defence at this point in time.

Supporters are saying the loss in east London was the worst away performance since Nuneaton on a bleak Tuesday night two seasons ago and, most worryingly, were critical of the perceived lack of effort shown by the players. I wasn't at the match and, it wasn't obvious from the commentary, but the fact that Simon Weaver came out and apologised to the travelling fans afterwards speaks volumes.

For the first time since I started writing this column, I must admit to being genuinely worried. Yes, we're only five matches in and there's a heck of a long way to go, but it seems that my pre-season hopes of another play-off challenge may have to be reassessed.

Good players don't become bad players overnight and we still have to put all of this into some sort of perspective. Town have no God-given right to be in the National League rubbing shoulders with all these ex-Football League teams, and certainly no god given right to be finishing sixth in it every season. We're here though, because we deserve to be. Yet the success we've seen has been as much down to hard work and application, as skill. The players have consistently left everything out on the pitch. Rest on your laurels, or be anything less than 100%, and this league will punish you.

Learning from all of this, maybe we need to go back to basics, reassess our expectations, and start digging in as a club to earn enough points to ensure we maintain our place in this league, first and foremost. Once that milestone has been achieved, anything else is a bonus.

One of the only positive things to come out of Dagenham at the weekend was Brendan Kiernan smashing in his first competitive goal in a Town shirt. He's been the success story from our new signings so far, seemingly doing everything but finding the back of the net in the opening four games. In an interview on Radio York following his man-of-the-match, yet penalty-missing, performance on the opening day, his undimmed enthusiasm shone through like a beacon. He just wanted to keep winning the ball, running at opposing defences and making things happen. That, in a nutshell, is exactly the attitude Town need going forward.

Two points and £2.72 disappear down the shute

Stockport County (H) W 2-1. Goals: Beck, Bradley. Crowd: 1,326. AFC Fylde (A) D 0-0. Crowd: 1,317. Article originally published on Thursday 29th August 2019 under the title *'We should be two points better off.'*

The coach is sitting impatiently in front of my house, as I'm scrabbling around looking for my suitcase upstairs. When I eventually find it, it's full of junk left over from my previous trip. I tip it out all over the floor, telling my wife that *'I'll clear it up when I get back,'* before joining the others on the coach. It's then I realise with horror that I haven't actually packed anything. A loud bleeping noise cuts through the morning. It's 6.30am. I groan and switch the alarm clock off. There's a dog to walk and an 8.30am coach to Lytham St Anne's to catch. I think this football lark's beginning to get to me. But more about that later.

I used to look forward to playing Stockport at Wetherby Road. That was until they thrashed us in the Trophy last season. This time around, however, it's a fairly even first half, both teams have chances but suffer from limp finishing. The bright spark for Town is the debut of Alex Bradley, he looks keen, finding space and wanting the ball. After the previous two home matches, I'm happy to get to half-time at nil all.

Town step it up a gear again after half-time though, dominating possession in a real dangerous spell. Falkingham dissects the entire Stockport defence with a slide rule pass to a marauding Fallowfield, who's first time cross is hammered in by Beck, barely two minutes after he'd put another one wide. He screams out his frustration in delight towards the Kop. Kiernan then brushes the post from a corner and Falkingham cuts in from the corner flag and hits a vicious, dipping shot that somehow the keeper pushes over, before undoing all his good work by being caught trying to play football in his own area, rather than pumping the ball into Row Z, sorry, Row C of the 1919 stand.

We look to have shot ourselves in the foot and I'm settling for the point, as Alex Bradley is announced man-of-the-match. The thoughts of some people around me are that it should go to Beck, but I don't agree. Then, in the 93rd minute, Kiernan audaciously takes down a ball he has no right to control, cuts inside, looks up and slides the ball into the path of the on-rushing Bradley who drives it into the corner of the net. *'He's definitely man-of-the-match now,'* states the bloke next to me after we've finished flinging ourselves around like lunatics. I make a mental note to get next week's lottery numbers off whoever chose man-of-the-match. How on earth did they know that was going to happen?

It's a massive three points for Town, wiping away the hurt of the previous three defeats, and we look much better with three in central midfield.

Two days later, Molly and I find ourselves on the beach at Lytham St Anne's. The sun's shining in Harrogate, but here at Lytham it's slightly overcast. This always happens when I put my shorts on. We're watching a match between Town and

Fylde supporters, bags down for goalposts, a result of a friendship that was struck up between the clubs a few years back.

I would take part, but I 'retired' twenty years ago having been taken out by a dodgy tackle on Woodhouse Moor, but that's a story for another day. Oh well, if you insist. I was playing in the Falkingham deep midfield role when the pitch opened up for me. Finding myself with just one defender between myself and the goal, I pushed the ball around her and went the other side, sensing glory and the adoration of my team-mates. It was then I was taken out by a crude elbow and had to retire with bruised ribs. I've played rarely since.

Fylde take the lead, although I think the ball went over the non-existent cross bar, before the game's stopped to allow a dangerous hole in the pitch to be filled. Town force their way back into it heroically, but Fylde win it with a cracker of a goal. Their defence then packs the square of sand in front of the goal to keep the valiant Town attack out. It sounds all too familiar and I can't even blame the referee, as he's a Town fan. He did, however, over-compensate for this by giving all the marginal decisions to our opponents.

After four hours at the seaside, during which time we lose our obligatory £2.72 in the 2p slot machines, our coach sets off for Mill Farm and arrives barely ten minutes before kick-off. From the off, something seems strange. There's very little atmosphere in the home end and Fylde are a shadow of the team they were last season. Even Danny Rowe is hitting free kicks tamely wide. Maybe we should give Town credit for handling them in a more mature way than the play-off match when we went two down in ten fateful minutes. Whatever,

I'm not complaining. If Town can step it up ten per cent in the second half, the Coasters are there for the taking.

It doesn't happen and the air of lethargy extends eventually to the normally boisterous Town fans. Then, after 73 fairly forgettable minutes, a moment of utter controversy causes a proper football match to break out.

Stead, on for Beck, capitalises on a shoddy back pass and slots in past the keeper right in front of us. The away end erupts and, when we've finished flinging ourselves around like lunatics again, something's not right. The ref points to his arm after discussions with the linesman and disallows the goal. We react in fury and bewilderment to what seems like the chalking off of a perfectly good goal. It feels like we've been VAR-ed.

It turns out that the ball brushed Stead's arm unintentionally on the way past him from the defender, and the delayed handball decision from the linesman is solely because Stead went on to place the ball in the net. If he hadn't, it wouldn't have been handball. Work that one out. Last season the goal would have stood. This season, under the new rule change, it's chalked off. The law is a complete ass. It doesn't help that the handball was so slight, that only the linesman seemingly saw it in real time.

The Town players seem incensed at the injustice of it all and lay siege to the home goal, hitting the woodwork for the second time and creating other chances, but it just won't go in. The officials leave the pitch to a chorus of *'It's a robbery,'* although, in reality, they probably think the law's lousy too. The Town players are applauded off by the travelling fans. Fylde really got away with one today.

Molly and I arrive home with the coach load of Town fans, including eighteen youngsters, shattered but happy. It's been a really great day out. Four points from the two bank holiday matches is a decent return, but it could and should have been six.

'... and you're supposed to be writing this up too'

Dover Athletic (H) L 0-2. Crowd: 900. Chorley (H) W 2-0. Goals: Kiernan, Muldoon. Crowd: 792. Article originally published on Thursday 5th September 2019 under the title *'Victory over Chorley a welcome tonic after our worst display in three years.'*

It's seventy minutes into the Chorley match on Tuesday night and I'm talking to a fellow supporter next to me in the Kop.

'I'll take one nil at this stage,' I say, as a period of sustained Chorley possession ensues and Town struggle to get out of their own half.

'But it's two nil,' says the man stood next to me, turning to look at me with a puzzled expression on his face.

'What?' I stutter, bemused, thinking I know it's not the most exciting of matches, but I'm sure I'd have remembered a second goal. I think he may be having me on.

'Muldoon scored,' he replies.

'Really? ... When?' More stuttering ensues.

'Yes, really. After forty seven minutes.'

I'm still not sure whether to believe him, so I take a sneaky Twitter peak on my phone. There it is in black and white, 2-0 in little brackets under the latest entry. I don't know whether to be happy or slightly annoyed that I missed it. My whole second half so far has been built on shifting sand.

[143]

'And you're supposed to be writing this up too,' he laughs. It's a fair point, well made, but the *Advertiser* did say they weren't after a match report every week, more a tale of the terraces. It's just as well.

It takes a while, but eventually my brain dissembles the truth.

I'd been in the 1919 bar at half-time, talking to Supporters' Club Secretary Paul Mitchell. He can talk, as can I. By the time I emerged, I thought the second half must surely have been underway, but had been pleasantly surprised to see that Chorley were just kicking off and Town fans were still filing around the ground towards the Kop. I'd heard Jack Muldoon's name announced to a round of applause, followed by the announcement of a Chorley substitution, so I'd assumed Jack had been subbed off at half-time.

Of course, with the benefit of hindsight, what I was witnessing was the restart following the second goal. It's a solid case of my brain taking two plus two and making five.

What makes things worse was various comments I'd uttered in the second half, such as *'Town have started slowly'* and, in response to the fellow supporter next to me commenting confidently that Town would win this easily, *'Are you sure? I'm not.'* He must have thought I was mad. Or at best, really, really pessimistic.

The final embarrassment though was realising that Muldoon was still on the pitch twenty minutes into the second half. In fairness, he hadn't seen the ball much down our end, and I stated as much. The withering look I got from my daughter Molly was indescribable.

Embarrassment aside, although we shouldn't get carried away, as struggling-at-the-bottom-of-the-table Chorley are pretty poor tonight, it's a vital and very welcome three points in a must-win game. Town haven't created a lot going forward, and the free flowing football of last season isn't quite there tonight, but it's a professional performance with a clean sheet and really pleasing to see the players get off to a quick goal-scoring start in each half. Myself and a few other stragglers in the 1919 excepted, of course.

The same can't be said of the Dover match at the weekend, where the consensus of opinion around me is that Town put in possibly their worst performance for three years. Dover were a very good, well-organised team with a dangerous centre forward, reducing Town to hitting the ball in the general direction of an isolated and unsupported Beck, only for it to keep coming straight back. The visitors forced us to play too deep and when we did venture forward, the players found it difficult to penetrate a well-marshalled Dover rearguard. Even the normally lively Kiernan was snuffed out by two or three visiting players every time he got the ball. With the crowd on a downward trajectory into three figures, under half of the attendance for the Dover home game last year, and the team seemingly indifferent on the pitch, the loudest chant from Town fans was, *'Eighteen quid and no one's here.'* It was ultimately depressing to watch and I'm glad Molly wasn't there to witness it, having made the right decision to go to a friend's party instead. Even the manager admitted he was bored after the game, whilst trying to reassure us that they don't practice hit and hope in training. I'll look forward to a different routine from the kick-off then in future.

It's an inconsistent start to the new season, summed up by one defeat and one win in two home matches. Thankfully the win over our Lancashire neighbours tonight takes us nearer to mid-table than the bottom in these early skirmishes, and that will do nicely for me.

Callum Howe (hidden) heading a late equaliser at Hartlepool, in our first away trip in the National League, August 2018. *(Matt Kirkham)*

Josh Falkingham salutes the Town end, as Howe piles on. *(Matt Kirkham)*

Joe Leesley pings in yet another dangerous cross at home to Chesterfield, November 2018. *(Matt Kirkham)*

Aaron Williams celebrates his 97th minute equaliser in the same match. *(Matt Kirkham)*

Joy in the Wetherby Road Stand on the final whistle. *(Matt Kirkham)*

Liam Kitching scores the winner to knock York City out of the FA Trophy, December 2018. *(Matt Kirkham)*

Mark Beck rises to head the third goal against Hartlepool in front of the TV cameras, January 2019. *(Matt Kirkham)*

Town equalise at Dover Athletic, February 2019. *(Matt Kirkham)*

Town players and fans celebrating the winning own goal at Chesterfield, February 2019. *(Matt Kirkham)*

A section of the family coach at Barrow, March 2019. *(Rich Hawley)*

Jack Muldoon retrieving the ball after pulling a goal back at Barrow. Note the two blurred figures, sharing a lone Twix, celebrating in the background. *(Matt Kirkham)*

Jack Muldoon surveys the aftermath of George Thomson's winning goal at Havant & Waterlooville, April 2019. *(Matt Kirkham)*

It's the Harrogate girls making all the noise. Molly and friends at the Gateshead match in front of the new stand, April 2019.

A water fight in the seats at Leyton Orient, April 2019. *(Jack Wilkinson)*

Town players in front of the 'Drunken Misfits' banner, as the Play-Off Quarter Final at AFC Fylde slips away, May 2019. *(Matt Kirkham)*

Goalmouth action from Town's 3-0 win at Barrow, August 2019.

AFC Fylde and Town supporters staging a football match on the beach at Lytham St. Annes, August 2019.

Lytham St. Annes, prior to the goalless draw at AFC Flyde.

Updating the photograph from three years ago, Molly at The Shay, Halifax, on a Tuesday night in September 2019.

Mark Beck losing his shirt versus Sutton United, September 2019. the referee gave a free kick to the visitors (of course).

Relax, it's only grass. I spent the day in bed, as Jon Stead gives a wry smile on the radio

Torquay United (A) L 2-4. Goals: Stead 2 (1 pen). Crowd: 2,527.
Article originally published on Thursday 12th September 2019
under the title *'Baffling, horrendous refereeing mistake compounds my food poisoning misery.'*

The Stray*, last Saturday, half an hour before kick off in Devon. A man stops a car, jumps out and empties the contents of his stomach onto the grass in front of him, bemused passers by giving him a wide berth. He briefly passes out, before coming round, not realising where he is at first, staggers unsteadily back to the car, emerges to be sick again, before eventually driving off for home.

Did I report a drunk driver? No, because that person was me, on the way back from Skipton with food poisoning, no drink having passed my lips since a solitary half pint a week ago at the Dover game. Please don't get too upset with me, custodians of the Stray. The grass will be getting some good biodegradable nutrients this week and the dog and I do a sterling job, until well into December each year, of picking up inconsiderately discarded sprinkler stems after the bonfire, thus preventing injury to all the young footballers on weekend mornings.

Subsequently, I crawled home and took myself to bed, missing the entire commentary from Torquay in the process. It probably saved my blood pressure from exceeding all safe limits.

Under normal circumstances, this would have been the week we were celebrating Town winning and converting, yes you heard right, scoring a penalty down in deepest Devon. This absolutely momentous event was rather overshadowed, though, by probably the most baffling and horrendous refereeing decision I've ever seen in all my years watching football.

Jon Stead, on a high having scored twice to kick-start his Town career, and on a booking for a culmination of minor offences in the first half, ran towards a Torquay player in the centre circle. As he did so, his opponent kicked the ball from close range and it flicked off his shoulder as he went towards the ball. Stead was facing towards his own goal at the time, the ball stayed in home possession, there was no advantage, nobody appealed, it was unavoidable, accidental. And it was not handball. The referee blew up immediately, went straight for his cards and sent him off, apparently shouting *'deliberate handball, deliberate handball.'* You can hear and see Stead saying *'It hit my shoulder,'* on the video, to no avail. Simon Weaver, in his after-match Radio York interview said that the referee had bizarrely pulled him aside at half-time, and issued a warning that Stead was already on a yellow. It appears that the referee, Mr Jackson, had already made his mind up.

After his unjustly disallowed goal at Fylde, I wouldn't blame Jon Stead if he came out swinging, but he fought back his frustration well and gave a wry smile at the unjust nature of the situation. If indeed you can give a wry smile on the radio. It was telling when he said that the one thing that had stood out for him since coming down to the National League was the poor standard of the refereeing.

Teams down to ten men can often be extremely hard to break down. Unfortunately this wasn't Town in Devon. Mitigating circumstances, definitely, but it's worth pointing out that Torquay were down to a make-shift, threadbare team, with all fit players utilised. I think the most disappointing thing for me was the third Torquay goal, Belshaw's penalty save popping back up nicely for the taker to score at the second attempt. The disappointing part was that three home players were the most advanced to take advantage of the rebound.

So, Town's second away 4-2 defeat in the first ten games finds them back down to seventeenth, but we live to fight again next week. Hopefully our luck will turn.

Watching the highlights back on the Town website, it's amazing how, in a crowd of two and a half thousand, all you can hear is the Town fans singing. A huge shout-out goes to the fifty nine fans who travelled down, many of them leaving at 6.30 in the morning. It may seem like a small amount to teams like Stockport and Notts County, but numbers have increased ten-fold since the Supporters Club started running coaches. Hopefully, it was a good trip, bar the result, but looking on the bright side... you didn't have me on the coach to contend with, food poisoning and all.

A 200-acre open grassland area encompassing part of Harrogate town centre. It's protected by an act of Parliament, and is something that the locals are extremely protective of.

Goodbye Joe... now, if only we had a player that can hit a decent cross

Boreham Wood (H) D 0-0. Crowd: 942. Article originally published on Thursday 19th September 2019 under the title *'Disappointment at Joe's departure and bore draw eased by ticket price u-turn.'*

On passing the door of our Project Manager's office this week, I'm summoned inside briefly. He knows a little thing or two about non-league football, having captained Farsley Celtic and Bradford Park Avenue until not so long ago.

'I hear Joe Leesley's gone out on loan. What's going on there?'

I tell him the tale of how Joe was dropped to the bench after starting the season so brightly, as Town reverted to a 4-3-3 formation in response to a couple of defeats. Now he's gone and asked for a loan move as he wants to play first team football as opposed to warming the bench.

My boss's reply is straight to the point, *'Town can't afford to lose a player like that in their position.'*

I find it very hard to disagree. 34 goals and 71 assists in 134 starts tells its own story.

I break the bad news to Molly and she's not happy either. We've been watching Joe ever since he joined Town from Alfreton, relieved when his rumoured move to Salford fell through a couple of seasons ago. The vivid memory of his swirling crosses landing on the head of Simon Ainge with a guided missile-like precision, his second half strike against Brackley in the play-offs, his visible frustration as a killer cross goes to waste, the anticipation as he runs up to swing in a dangerous corner, and not forgetting that pearl of a goal against Solihull this season. All of this, and more, is etched into my memory and I don't want it to end here.

His crossing ability and set-piece delivery from wide has been a major contributor to Town finishing as top scorers in the league for the last two seasons. Yes, he's not great at taking people on and getting to the line, neither was David Beckham, but like Beckham, he has that knack of slinging over a dangerous cross or hitting a great set piece to change a game.

I could say, it feels like we've lost a family member, but that would be a little melodramatic. Maybe it's more like seeing your child going away to college for the first time, or undergoing a trial separation with your long term partner. Whatever, I hope you get my point, we're going to miss him and hope he returns to the fold soon.

Hence it's a slightly subdued Molly and I heading to Wayside Walk to meet her two friends prior to the Boreham Wood match. Try as I might, I can't spin this match out into anything resembling exciting. Boreham would be the word. It starts off positively, both teams creating chances early on, but soon descends into a non-event for a long period either side of half-time. Town can take the positive of a clean sheet, although they again have Belshaw to thank for keeping it that way. The other bright spot is the performance and confidence on the ball of loanee Alex Bradley, returning to central midfield after being crocked at Fylde. Other than that, it's pretty slim pickings as Town lack a little bit of confidence and a cutting edge going forward, often overplaying on the edge of the area. I find myself thinking *'If only we had a player that can hit a decent cross ...'*

The goalless draw's about right and, seeing as Boreham Wood could have won it late on, I'll settle for that. Town have the sense of a team still struggling to decide on its best formation and injuries to key midfielders haven't helped in this regard. It's a work in progress and hopefully it'll get there.

Before events overtook me, I was actually planning to address the issue of ticket prices and falling attendance figures this week. We'll never know how much of an effect the increased ticket prices are having on attendance figures, but there are plenty of stories out there of people who've been put off from attending Town matches due to the admission cost. One of my work colleagues, who attended maybe eight games last season with his son, is one of those people. For him, it's reached the tipping point where the cost of going outweighs the benefits.

Of course you've got to add other factors into the mix, such as the success this season of Leeds and York, the fact that Town are eighteenth and struggling to play the consistent eye-pleasing football of the last two seasons, and possibly the loss of the Wetherby Road stand to home regulars for many home games. The case remains though, that ticket prices are playing their part.

Following the Club's statement on the subject in the *Advertiser* a couple of weeks ago, the Supporters Club wrote the following letter to managing director Gary Plant.

'We wanted to contact you again about ticket price increases after your Advertiser interview in which you

expressed your first concern in public about falling attendances.

The following are points already made (and apparently discarded) before, but are crucial to the problem:

There needs to be an acceptance that prices have gone up more than £2. Most people paying match-by-match last season used the facility to get their ticket for £14. Now their decision is whether to pay £18. That's an increase of £4.

Supporters are grateful for the investment in ground improvements, but that expenditure is in the past. All that's relevant now for decision-making purposes is you have space for up to 4,000 people to watch each game, and each extra fan that comes in will cost the club very little, but often purchase food, drink and merchandise on top of their ticket revenues.

The stiffest increases will have been felt by those who have fallen foul of the new concessions policies. Reverting to last season's categories would surely succeed in tempting some of these people back.

The current ticketing policy is making the club LESS sustainable because revenues are falling. We urge you to cut ticket prices (including balancing concessions for existing season ticket holders) before attendances and revenues fall further.'

The club's response this last week has been to reinstate £2 reductions on advance tickets, and for that they should be given some credit. I'm sure we haven't heard the last of it, and I'm sure I'll be touching on the subject again, but our short term priority now as supporters must be to get behind the team going forward.

I, for one, don't want this crazy National League adventure to end.

'Second in the league, they're having a laugh...'

Maidenhead United (A) D 1-1. Goal: Jones. Crowd: 1,127. FC Halifax Town (A) W 1-0. Goal: Beck. Crowd: 1,918. Article originally published on Thursday 26th September 2019 under the title *'The pessimist in me is proved wrong as our unbeaten run at The Shay continues.'*

It's an early finish for me at a rain-deluged workplace today. I head back to Harrogate to walk the dog, before heading off to drop my wife at her parents' house in Halifax whilst Molly and I head down to the Shay. A brief stop in Bradford for some chips and we're in the ground with five minutes to spare. Admission prices here are daylight robbery. It's £20 for me and £9 for Molly. An eye-watering amount seeing as many Halifax folk won't be awash with spare cash in these difficult times.

The pessimist in me isn't expecting a lot in a damp West Yorkshire tonight. The home team have started the season in fine form, sitting second in the table, having scored plenty of goals in the process. If there's a chink of light for Town, it's that our hosts have lost two of their last three.

As Molly's keen to remind me, we haven't seen Town lose at The Shay in our previous two visits. The first of those visits, four seasons ago, was her maiden away match following Town. I have a picture of her beaming away in the seats that day, following Jack Emmett's winner. We recreate that picture tonight, and I realise how much she's grown up in the interim period.

It's a good first half for Town, save for a fifteen minute spell when Belshaw twice brilliantly thwarts McAlinden, their danger man. The second save is an instinctive block with his foot after a low free kick evades the defensive wall. Town, however, come close a number of times. Bradley hits a curling shot that tests the keeper, Burrell crashes a drive against the angle of post and crossbar, Beck has a downward header tipped round the post and Fallowfield has a first goal in heaven knows how many years chalked off for offside.

It seems a strangely muted atmosphere inside the Shay, empty on two sides, amongst the decent turnout of nineteen hundred home fans. Just imagine how many they could attract if they lowered the ticket prices. And just imagine the noise the Town fans could make if they had that number. Maybe it's just me, but I expected the place to be rocking, what with their team being second in the table and all that.

The muted home atmosphere off the pitch, seems to have spread to the home team on it, and the second half appears to be petering out to a goalless draw. A great result for Town, but I'm thinking that we really need to be picking up three points at some stage, as every draw seems to send us a place down the table.

The eighty five Town fans are running through a full repertoire of songs, although 'Is this a library?' seems slightly inaccurate, as you can make a noise in libraries these days. With the UCI World Championships closing down roads in Harrogate for the week, 'Town full of teashops' morphs wonderfully into 'We're just a town full of lycra.'

Halifax have more possession around the Town box, but a gritty, closing-down defensive performance keeps them at arms' length. Three games and only one goal conceded so far, all without Falkingham too. All of a sudden, things don't look quite so bad.

Then, out of the blue in the 89th minute, a flowing move straight out of last season, between Fallowfield and the recalled Thomson on the right wing, leads to confusion in the home box. The ball falls to Beck and he unbelievably stabs home from an acute angle right in front of us.

The Town section erupts into an explosion of flying limbs and the players run over to celebrate, Beck sliding onto his chest in front of us. There's no time left for Halifax to come back, although Muldoon finds time to miss, when put clean through at the death. No matter. The whistle goes and the celebrations can begin in earnest.

'Why do we always lose to pub teams?' moans one Halifax fan to his mate on the way out.

'Second in the league, they're having a laugh,' I say very loudly and pointedly to Molly as we walk past them. Our unbeaten record at the Shay remains intact.

Town full of lycra, we're just a town full of lycra...

Sutton United (H) W 2-0. Goals: Thomson, Muldoon (pen). Crowd: 769. Article originally published on Thursday 3rd October 2019 under the title *'Half-time chips, a solid back four and even a spot-kick conversion to enjoy.'*

'Who put the ball in the Halifax net? Marky flipping Beck did!'

After Tuesday night's heroics, the Town fans have a new song. I've softened it for *Advertiser* approval, of course, but you get the gist.

As a fellow supporter pointed out to me after the win in a sodden West Yorkshire, not only did Beck put the ball in the Halifax net, he did so after running the length of the pitch, having started the move by heading the ball out to Alex Bradley from his own six yard box.

Today Town are unfairly competing with the Cycling World Championships, barely half a mile down the road, but we wouldn't be anywhere else. With no segregation, we're back in the Wetherby Road stand, Sutton United are in town and it feels like home.

Thomson's lightning break of an opening goal is again a result of Beck tackling an opponent on the edge of our area following a corner and feeding Bradley lurking in midfield. It's a borderline foul but the referee plays on, much to the surprise of some of Sutton's players and, indeed, myself. History isn't quite repeated here though, as the speed of the move leaves Beck with the visitors' central defence way back down the pitch. Having seen Thomson out of sorts pre-season and then out of the squad and watching from the away end at Fylde, it's good to see him restored in the team and heading back towards his best.

It's a devastating counter attacking goal, coming after a spell in which the visitors were beginning to look the most likely, and I head to the Club Shop at half-time in a decent mood. I'm there to collect two old Town programmes from under the counter for the princely sum of fifty pence each. There's an Alex Bradley centre-spread in both of them and Molly's friends have a slight crush on him. We even manage to get chips. A couple of weeks ago we had to look on in envy as twenty-odd Boreham Wood fans had the snack bar in the Wetherby Road Stand to themselves. By the time the horrendous queues at the Kop end snack bar died down, everything was sold out.

After the break, Sutton probe for an equaliser at the 1919 end, as Town are forced into playing on the counter. The defence holds firm though, as Connor Hall and Will Smith seem to be building up a good understanding after a slightly rocky start to the season. Smith impresses with a number of vital interceptions, whilst Hall is rock solid in the air. In fairness though, the whole team is putting in a shift. Burrell's move back to central midfield is welcome, if long overdue. At this rate, our captain will struggle to get back in the team.

Then disaster strikes. All the good work appears to have been undone as George Smith accidentally clatters into a Sutton attacker in the area. Up steps central defender and captain Collins, scorer of the penalty that dumped Leeds out of the Cup two and a half years ago. And more importantly, scorer of a last minute penalty at the same end last season to cruelly deny Town a win in their maiden National League match. Not so this time though. Belshaw gets down brilliantly to his left to push the penalty away, and Town survive.

For me it's justice done, as Collins spends much of the match either holding onto Beck's shirt or pushing down into his neck. I take a random picture of a corner kick in the second half, as you do, and Beck looks like he's playing with no shirt on, it's being pulled so much. Not that I've been staring at it, of course, but both the referee and linesman are looking in that direction. What on earth do they see?

Justice is further served as Beck assists the second goal too. This time it's a route one flick off his head from Belshaw that puts Muldoon in behind the static Sutton central defence, one-on-one, right in front of us. He takes a heavy first touch, the keeper dives in and gets a hand to the ball, pushing it out wide. Muldoon makes absolutely no attempt to avoid the keeper's outstretched arm, shall we say, and then coolly dispatches the resulting spot kick. Oh how good that last bit sounds after our penalty travails of the early part of the season.

We're up to mid-table, unbeaten in four and looking more solid at the back, if a little less prolific up front. Let's hope we can build on this next Saturday evening when the TV cameras and Ebbsfleet roll into Town.

Housework precedes a routine win and a rare goal against Wrexham

Ebbsfleet United (H) W 2-0. Goals: Kiernan 2. Crowd: 747. Wrexham (A) D 1-1. Goal: Fallowfield. Crowd: 3,435. Article originally published on Thursday 10th October 2019 under the title *'An upturn in fortunes out on the pitch but attendance figures remain an issue.'*

It's Saturday. Early afternoon. Lunch eaten. I'm washing up and looking forward to a leisurely free afternoon stretching ahead of me, as Town aren't kicking off until twenty past five.

'The stairs need vacuuming when you've finished, Molly's room too. Then there's the apples to get down off the tree... and don't forget the dog pee stain in the front room.' Doh.

Now, not even I can pretend that the visit of bottom placed Ebbsfleet to Wetherby Road is a major draw for the neutral BT Sport audience, but it's a chance to break into the top half of the table for Town.

The visiting team should find themselves two or three down after twenty five minutes, as Town play with a high intensity and purpose from the off. It threatens to have all the making of one of those matches where the visiting team mugs you with a breakaway goal, against the run of play, as Town fail to take advantage of some brilliant approach play and chances. Thankfully, Ebbsfleet aren't that good going forward, and Kiernan wins the game with two clinical goals. The first a great finish from a tight angle after taking it round the keeper, although I must admit I thought he'd taken it too wide initially, and the second an instinctive header from a neat Town move, against the run of play early in the second half. After that, with the game safe, things kind of fizzle out. It's a solid win all the same.

It's a strange feeling listening to the Radio York commentary from North Wales on Tuesday night. Barry Parker's ill, so we have the York City commentary team standing in to witness a well-earned point for Town at a place that yielded two disappointing defeats last season. It's Jack Diamond who changes the dynamic of the match when he comes on, creating the equalising goal and unnerving Wrexham by simply running at them.

What makes it interesting though, is the York City commentators' perspective on Town. They pass comment on the noticeable difference in quality between the National League and National League North (mind the gap, York City), and the frenetic pace of the game. Although pointing out that Town didn't create enough chances for all their clever build-up play and that the final ball was sometimes lacking, they seem impressed by the team overall, especially in the sense that they didn't give up, ran for ninety minutes and *looked a really competent team, fit, strong, knowing their jobs.'* Praise indeed, and I think that adequately sums up the main improvement in Town now the squad has started to gel.

I'll even forgive them for mistakenly referring to Harrogate as *'Halifax'* on at least two occasions, but not for stating that maybe we'd be happy taking a point back up to West Yorkshire. I'd just like to remind them that we're currently the top team in NORTH Yorkshire.

It's a week of two halves for me though, with the positivity on the pitch tempered by an attendance of 742 off the pitch for the Ebbsfleet televised match; half the number for the corresponding match last season. The home attendance only dipped below 1,100 once last season, and was often much, much higher, but we're now on a run of five consecutive home games with the crowd well down into three figures. To put this into some form of perspective, the last few turnouts have been at the level of attendances in the National League North, four seasons ago, when we finished mid-table. It feels like a step backwards.

One of the most exciting aspects of watching Town over the last few seasons has been witnessing the momentum building and the attendances growing, as Town have gone higher than they've ever been before, whilst playing an attractive brand of football. The club has played no little part in this, doing great work in the community and attracting interest in the club. All of this makes the sudden dip in attendances hard to take, especially as this bunch of players deserves to play in front of bigger crowds.

I think we can now say that the decision to increase prices has been a bit of an own goal, a fact acknowledged by the recent price decreases on advance tickets, introduced by the club, and we're down to the 'hardcore' at the moment. Albeit a level of hardcore support that was unthinkable a few years ago.

It shows that you can't take your supporters for granted in a town that doesn't have a reputation for being a football town, and the additional pounds gained from the once a season visits from Wrexham or Notts County fans doesn't benefit the club, when home turnstile income is down by more than the cash generated from the aforementioned away fans.

Although the recent price decrease is a move in the right direction, it may prove tricky to get fans back through the gate once they've decided to go elsewhere. Now that the cyclists and Sky TV have left town, and the team's on a six match unbeaten run, maybe that tide will start to turn. Time will tell.

I'd suggest that the club needs to go back to square one to try and attract more fans back in through the gates. Reintroducing at least one match with free admission would be a good start, and what about a half-season ticket? Let's get those fans in, give them a great experience and hope they come back. Reducing ticket prices drastically for kids, and making great efforts to attract them in, would also be a positive move. Every youngster attending the match brings at least one adult with them and this breeds the fans of the future. My daughter Molly's a prime example of this. And she's here this evening with two of her friends, bucking the trend. They've both turned into Town fans and I must admit that I didn't see that coming, but £8 each on the day is still way too much for two unwaged fourteen year olds.

If you're reading this and don't come down to Wetherby Road very often, I'd urge you to make the effort and take another punt. Premier League it isn't, but it's real, honest and exciting, and all the better for it. It's certainly got to be better than vacuuming the stairs on a Saturday afternoon.

Next week: On The Road With Town. Your intrepid twosome undertake a difficult trip to the West Country.

These things take time.
A long trip to Yeovil
and hot-buttered toast

Yeovil Town (A) W 2-1. Goals: Kiernan, Muldoon. Crowd: 2,237.
Article originally published on Thursday 17th October 2019 under
the title *'A victory as fine as anything that I have witnessed during my
time as a Town fan.'*

'Molly, it's 5.35!' I shout up the stairs, in between rubbing
my bleary eyes, wondering whose clever idea this was.

'Yes dad, I'm already up,' comes the unexpectedly bright
reply from my normally impossible-to-get-up-on-a-weekend
teenager.

By the time I've emerged from the bathroom, Molly's
already downstairs and excitedly making hot-buttered toast
for us both. I think I've woken up in a parallel universe.

Come 6.30 and we're on a full coach load of Town
supporters bound for deepest Somerset. It's our first long
southern trip together and the second-longest trip of the
season, nudging Dover into third place by two miles, if Google
Maps is to be believed.

I've had my eye on the Yeovil trip ever since the fixtures
were announced, but I'll be the first to admit that the main
catalyst for going is the kind offer from Strata to pay for the
coach. I like a freebie.

It's a fairly uneventful six hour journey down and we arrive in Yeovil town centre at 12.30. Whilst the majority of the coach disperses into Wetherspoons next to the bus station, Molly and I hit the town. Well ok, the local Record Emporium, where I proceed to almost bore Molly to death whilst flicking through the racks of secondhand vinyl. Feeling guilty, I take her to Burger King to make up for it.

We head back to Wetherspoons for a quick half and a glass of tap water, before heading off to the ground. The original, historic Huish with it's famous eight feet sloping pitch lost the fight to Tesco in 1990, so our destination is a newer stadium built on the edge of town. It's still a great football stadium though and, with over 3,000 fans in attendance, it has the feel and atmosphere of a Football League ground. Unlike Halifax, Yeovil have a sizeable, boisterous choir behind the goal and, with the home team on a run of eight wins in nine, this could turn out to be quite a battle for Town.

Just before kick-off, I turn to Molly and she's in fits of uncontrollable laughter. It turns out that Yeovil's mascot, Jolly Green Giant, has lost his footing coming off the pitch and is now lying down, surrounded by the coaching staff from both teams. Thankfully he/she eventually picks themselves up gingerly and limps away to the stand, albeit a little less jolly.

Town proceed to emulate the mascot early doors; one or two players losing their footing on the slippery pitch, whilst Yeovil attack dangerously and at pace. The players manage to nullify the home threat though and gradually find a foothold in the game, so much so that they enjoy the bulk of possession for the last twenty five minutes of the first half. All you can hear is *'Yellow and Black Army'* from the sixty travelling fans with our new banner reading *'For The Love,*

Not The Glory'. The Yeovil end has gone quiet, and we delight in pointing that out. It's an encouraging sign.

Despite this, Yeovil have the best chance when Duffus, yes you read that right, breaks though one-on-one with Belshaw. He shoots through the Harrogate stopper's legs, although Belly manages to get a slowing touch on the ball. It's still heading for the net and 1-0 when Hall appears from nowhere to hack it off the line.

The start of the second half sees a mini-onslaught of the Town goal, as Yeovil attack towards their own fans. Another one's hacked away from the line, but apart from that, Town hold firm with a number of great blocks and clearing headers. Sixty five minutes gone and goalless. I'll take that.

Town weather the storm again and grow steadily into the second half. Then joy, as a Kiernan low shot-cum-cross trickles its way in slow motion into the far corner past the massed ranks of the home defence. Yeovil are shaken, they try to play out from the back like Barcelona, but it turns out they're Arsenal in disguise. A high pressing Beck intercepts from the centre back, slides the ball to Muldoon and it's 2-0 with twelve minutes to play. The wheels have come off for the Somerset side and you can hear a pin drop in the home end. Town go for the jugular against a home side on the ropes, but can't get a third.

With five added minutes left, the Town fans walk down to the front, ready to celebrate with the players. It's then that Yeovil finally breach the Town rearguard. Nerves set in. Have we been too cocky? But Town hold out comfortably for a win that compares with anything during my time watching them: Brackley Play-Off Final, York home and away, Halifax and Chesterfield away included.

The Yeovil boss, in a severe case of sour grapes, later accuses Town of *'spoiling the 3,200 fans' afternoon, because they don't really want to join in with you and play a game of football.'* How little he knows us. Whilst agreeing with him that we spoilt their fans' afternoon, after all we're not there to roll over and give them a ninth win in ten, he's otherwise way off the mark. Town setting up with two strikers and two wide midfielders and looking to attack at every opportunity, not sit on a lead, isn't negative. It's just that they've tightened up when not in possession of the ball and have recently blossomed into a team that can do the ugly closing down part of the game just as well as the passing and attacking part.

We eventually arrive back in Harrogate at 11:30pm, 550 miles later, both tired and emotionally drained, but happy. It's been a brilliant day, and I only wished we had the time to do it more often. Somehow, I don't think there's much chance of Molly making me hot-buttered toast tomorrow morning.

Footnote: I'd like to dedicate this column to Barry Parker, our brilliant Radio York commentator, who is currently undergoing an operation and heard his name being chanted on the radio whilst listening to the match in hospital. Get well soon, Barry, we miss your dulcet tones and dry sense of humour.

Can we play you every week? (part one)

FC Halifax Town (A) (FA Cup Fourth Qualifying Round) W 2-1. Goals: Beck 2. Crowd: 1,241. Article originally published on Thursday 24th October 2019 under the title *'Who put the ball in the Shaymen's net to set up dream FA Cup clash with Pompey?'*

We're singing in the away seats at Halifax for the third time this year. It's the FA Cup Fourth Qualifying Round. Town are 2-1 up and successfully holding our West Yorkshire rivals at bay, on the back of a seven match unbeaten run with four victories in the last five. Can life possibly get any better?

Then from behind us for several minutes, an angry voice rises, *'Come on Weaver, make a substitution! Useless! Do you know what you're doing? TAKE THE FRONT TWO OFF!'* Or words to that effect. Some people are never happy.

After a while, Molly turns to me and says *'I hope Weaver doesn't make a substitution now and we win with the same players on the pitch.'* She's inherited my stubborn streak sure enough, but I share her pain. It's quite a concession on her part though, seeing as Jack Emmett's on the bench.

'Who put the ball in the Shaymen's net?'

Let me take you back to 3pm. Town fans are buoyantly reminding Halifax fans of the last time we met, three weeks ago, and so are the players, taking the game to the home side in probably the best half of football I've seen them play this season. It's partly due to Town wanting it more and partly due to the fact that the Shaymen are standing off, applying no pressure to the Town players on the ball. I said it three weeks ago, and I'll say it again, how on earth are Halifax top of the table? Town really do have nothing to fear this season.

We're eight minutes in and Beck takes advantage of Kiernan wreaking havoc down the right wing. It's one of those immensely satisfying goals, as he reacts first, smashing the loose, bouncing ball high into the net, after the home keeper heroically tips a goal-bound header from his own defender onto the crossbar.

'*Who put the ball in the Shaymen's net? Twice!*' we roar in the away end.

Oh to be a fly on the wall in the home dressing room at half-time, as Halifax come back out like a team that's had the hairdryer treatment. Five passes into the restart and it's level at 1-1, Town's first touch of the ball is Belshaw picking it out of the net. The Shaymen should put another couple away in a frantic spell as Town buckle. Then, out of the blue, ten minutes in, another great piece of play down the right gets Muldoon in behind the home defence and he squares for Beck to sweep the ball in. Who else?

'*Who put the ball in the Shaymen's net? Thrice!*'

It's a goal very similar in build-up to his winner here in the league three weeks ago, and you can see the Halifax players' heads drop. Sure enough, substitutions duly made, Town safely see the match out to the sheer joy of the impressive turnout of 228 travelling fans. '*Que sera, sera, whatever will be, will be, we're going to Wemb-er-lee,*' rings out around a rapidly emptying Shay. Not that it was too full to start with as, despite a welcome reduction in admission prices, home fans only number thirteen over a thousand. The players come across to celebrate with us in front of the away section and we exit, looking forward to the First Round draw.

Now, if you're looking for an indicator as to how far Town have come in the last few years, then look no further than this. Time was, getting to the FA Cup First Round was a great achievement, following a lengthy cup run, now it's one match and we're there. Mind you, drawing the top team in the National League two seasons on the trot hasn't made it easy progress.

So, it's in a shared state of excitement, tinged with nervousness, that Molly and I sit down on Monday evening to watch the First Round Draw live on the BBC, something I haven't done for more years than I care to remember, and something Molly has never done. The Beeb's at Maldon & Tiptree FC and, after establishing that the stock answer to *'Who do you want in the next round?'* is *'The bye,'* the draw finally gets underway.

We're not hopeful, fully expecting a long wait, to then draw someone like Dover or Eastleigh away from home, when seventh ball in, out comes Town's ball.

'Number sixty, Harrogate Town, eighth in the National League, will play...'

Time slows, I can hear my heart thumping.

'...Portsmouth.'

Portsmouth. It takes a moment to sink in. Wow! Simply wow! Life just got appreciably better.

Wild abandon as Fiery Jack shoots down visitors and Town shut up shop

Aldershot Town (H) W 1-0. Goal: Emmett. Crowd: 1,507. Barnet (H) W 2-1. Goals: G. Smith, Muldoon. Crowd: 1,121. Article originally published on Thursday 31st October 2019 under the title 'Unbeaten in 10 and a big FA Cup tie on the horizon makes it a great time to be a Town fan.'

It's undoubtedly a great time to be a Town fan. Six points from two home games this week, ten games unbeaten, up to fourth in the National League, only four points off top spot, a dream cup tie against Portsmouth to look forward to and there's genuinely a buzz about the place again. This, however, only tells half the story.

After a fairly ordinary first period against Aldershot on Saturday, with the few chances created going begging at both ends, the second half descends into stalemate. With the visitors looking more likely, I find myself turning to Molly and wishing for substitutions. My point is that fresh players off the bench will bust a gut to make an impression ahead of the big Portsmouth cup tie. The manager must be thinking the same thing and throws on Thomson, Emmett and Stead in search of the win.

It's only then that a valiant and well-disciplined Aldershot side decide to settle for a point, as Town manage to work up a head of steam possession-wise, with all three subs looking lively. The game still seems to be heading towards a frustrating stalemate, until Emmett finds himself in the right place at the right time, one minute into injury time, slamming a knockdown from Will Smith into the roof of the net. He tears off gleefully towards the camera, one finger raised in delight. It happens right in front of us at the Kop end and, as dejected Aldershot players collapse to the floor, cursing and holding collective heads in hands, we jump around in wild abandon in front of them. This game can be so cruel. The previous ninety minutes are quickly forgotten. Oh how we love a last minute winner! Roll on Tuesday.

Barnet on Tuesday night turns out to be a strange one. Town enter it with confidence high, seeking to blow the visitors away with some great passing football and two goals in the first twenty minutes. When George Smith breezes through to smash in his debut Town goal, it looks like we could be in for a rout tonight. Then a long enforced water break for a Barnet injury around the thirty minute mark seemingly changes the entire flow of the game.

The visitors pull one back, before proceeding to pass the ball around with ease and not a little menace, as Town struggle to get anywhere near it for the rest of the first half. This pattern continues after the break, as Town seemingly lose the ability to put two passes together and Barnet are unrecognisable from the first thirty minutes. We're in the Kop end, but all the action is in the opposing half. I don't recall a single Town shot in front of us, as I spend the entire second half biting my nails and staring into the distance, our forwards only sporadically advancing past the half way line.

Thankfully, the manager brings on those fresh legs again in the form of Thomson and Stead to try and force Town up field. I'm figuring both players will again be hungry to make an impression ahead of the cup tie. What happens next beggars belief.

I'd already been admiring Town's self-control in the first half. An example of this being when Falkingham lost the ball in midfield and, instead of flying into the tackle to try to gain possession back, he and Fallowfield stayed on their feet to close down the man on the ball.

Not so Jon Stead. In his eagerness to win the ball having over run it, two minutes after coming on, he flies in two footed on a Barnet defender and it all kicks off on the pitch. There's no malice, but it's a reckless challenge. Down goes a second defender in the ensuing melee, as if he's been shot. After a long consultation with his linesman, the referee brandishes red to Stead and then flourishes his yellow card three times. Now we're really up against it.

It turns into a game of attack versus defence, as the entire Town team sits back waiting for Barnet to advance towards the area, before Burrell eventually intercepts the ball and boots it out towards the half-way line. There's no pretence of following it up the pitch now, as the entire Town team sits back waiting for Barnet to attack again. Will Smith eventually intercepts, boots it out and Town sit back waiting for Barnet to attack again... This loop plays continuously for the last fifteen minutes. To us in the Kop end, it feels like fifteen hours. The loop being broken only in the last minute of a torturous six additional minutes when the visitors finally break through the massed ranks, only for our magnificent last line of defence, Belshaw, to deny them brilliantly. Twice. There will be no repeat of Torquay away. My over-riding feeling is relief when the referee finally blows his whistle.

So, two wins for Town, neither straightforward or convincing, but I'll happily take six points. Both of these matches may well have been lost or drawn last season, but our new found tenacity in defence is turning those defeats and draws into wins, even though we're not scoring as many. It's a team unrecognisable from the one that displayed such defensive vulnerability in the early part of the season.

Footnote: At half-time in the Aldershot match, I lurk in the 1919 end and watch a group of lads from St Aidan's School take it in turn to hit penalties at one of their mates in goal. Whilst swinging to kick, one lad's shoe flies off. Quick as a flash, before the goalie even has time to laugh, he plants the ball into the net with his socked foot. It's a pretty impressive feat, especially as his shoe went in too.

Another lad stands ready to take his penalty and points to the left hand side of the keeper. 'I'm putting it there...' he says. Of course the keeper dives the other way, bluff well and truly accepted, as the penalty taker proceeds to put it exactly where he told the keeper he was going to put it. It's clever, and also very funny, although I wouldn't recommend it to Jack Muldoon as a strategy for taking penalties.

It's heart-warming to see this group of lads enjoying themselves, but they're also here to honour the memory of their brave friend, Frank Ashton, who tragically died from a rare form of bone cancer in February this year. The collection for Frank's Fund, a charity started to raise money for research into this rare form of bone cancer, raises over £500. It's a reminder that, as much as we agonise over this game of football, some things in life are much more important.

Bradford Park Avenue form low key support act to Portsmouth

Eastleigh (A) L 2-4. Goals: Kiernan, Muldoon. Crowd: 1,592. Bradford Park Avenue (H) (West Riding County Cup) W 2-1. Goals: Stead 2 (1 pen). Crowd: 112. Article originally published on Thursday 7th November 2019 under the title *'Few complaints as unbeaten run comes to an end with Portsmouth on horizon.'*

So much for the optimism of last week's column and the praise for Town's defensive performance over recent weeks. Victory at sixteenth placed Eastleigh would have lifted Town into third place in the league, but we've already established that there are no easy games in this league, and it appears that the collective wheels fell off down in deepest Hampshire.

A needless penalty, two players left unmarked at the back post and two absolute defensive howlers led to Town coming away on the wrong end of a 4-2 score line. It was a poor performance according to many of the 21 brave souls who made the long journey down there, bringing back memories of games at Dagenham and Torquay earlier in the season.

Overall though, we can't complain too much about our ten match unbeaten run coming to an end. It wasn't going to last forever, and I'm personally quite pleased with six points out of nine since the Portsmouth ball appeared out of the bag on the BBC. It quite often happens that a team's form dips in the approach to a big cup tie, as heads are, understandably, often elsewhere.

Simon Weaver's decision to start playing Warren Burrell in his best position in central midfield has been a major factor in the recent run, and it's no coincidence that Town haven't been as dominant in midfield in the last three games since Hall's injury and Warren's restoration into central defence. We got away with it against Aldershot and Barnet, but our luck finally ran out at Eastleigh.

Having not travelled down to Hampshire, Molly, her friend Lucy and I decide to get our football fix on a cold, damp Monday night. Bradford Park Avenue are the visitors in the West Riding County Cup and we're encouraged by the fact that Town are starting a strong team. The midfield of Kerry, Emmett, Thomson and Brown could easily be a first team midfield on a different day, highlighting the current strength of our squad in this area. Tellingly, the defence consists of players from the under 21s. Tonight's two man attack of Stead and Jones meanwhile, pays testament to the form of Muldoon and Beck.

It's not segregated, as the crowd is a sparse 112, so we take our favoured place in the Wetherby Road Stand amongst thirty or so other regulars. Whilst the travellers to Eastleigh can claim to be super fans, we can lay claim to being hardcore tonight!

The visitors sit rock bottom of the National League North, so we're hopeful of a good performance and a few goals. So much for optimism. Bradford have five first teamers and a series of nippy youngsters starting, and they're more than a match for Town tonight, even having the audacity to take the lead. Thankfully, Stead replies quickly, and we reach half-time level. It's not been a thriller, on or off the pitch, and I think the girls weren't quite expecting the low key nature of the affair.

The second half descends into a rather dreary contest. Town eventually getting their noses in front via a Stead penalty, awarded for a harsh handball decision. The only other exciting incident involves Bradford's stocky number five telling Town fans behind the goal to *'shut up'* in no uncertain terms, as one of their young players is given a bit of stick for going down after a slightly naughty challenge from Jones. It's funny, but I have much sympathy, as the visiting player's forced to hobble off the pitch and Bradford see the match out with ten men, having used all their substitutes. It's all a far cry from the cup tie fast approaching next Monday night.

As the visit of Portsmouth nears, one of the biggest talking points amongst the regulars is whether the club will confiscate the famous Pompey bell. One of the stranger sights the previous Tuesday evening against Barnet was watching a steward taking away the drum from the fans in the Kop. There's currently a ban on drums at night matches after complaints from local residents. When this ban was first introduced at Town a couple of years ago, it actually led to a protest from the fans, as many refused to come out from the 1919 bar to support the team in the second half. Not a great hardship, admittedly.

Personally I prefer the approach of Wolves fans many years ago at Wigan in the old Fourth Division. It was the late eighties and Wigan were relative newcomers to the Football League. The away end, obviously constructed when visits from the likes of Shepshed and Mossley were commonplace, consisted of a few oval rows of terracing in front of a large grass bank with a structure partially resembling a bike shed built on top of it. A couple of thousand Wolves fans turned up in party mood with a football, having seen promotion achieved a week before, and an impromptu pre-match kick about ensued on the grass bank, before a lone policeman confiscated the ball. There then proceeded to unfold one of the most farcical sights I've ever witnessed at a football ground as, quick as a flash, the away fans formed a conga behind the by now, red-faced copper, appealing for him to throw the ball back. He didn't cave into the pressure, however, delivering the ball safely to his superior.

The drum ban at Town is made all the more bizarre by the fact that the PA system pumps out music and announcements before, during and after the match at stun volume inside the ground. Not that I'm complaining though, far from it. Having set off very late for the match the other night, I still managed to pick up the team line-ups from half a mile away near St. Aidan's.

There is a light that sometimes goes out. Blue Monday as Pompey edge out Town

Portsmouth (H) (FA Cup First Round) L 1-2. Goal: Beck. Crowd: 3,408. Article originally published on Thursday 14th November 2019 under the title *'Disappointment at not beating Pompey shows just how far Town have come.'*

'That's why I wanted to leave at 6.30' I tell Molly, as we view the size of the queue down Wetherby Road. We're only quarter of an hour behind schedule and, in fairness, Molly's friends turned up at our house bang on time. I'm the one who wasn't ready.

We join the long snake of people outside the ground on Wetherby Road and, ten minutes later, haven't moved an inch. I've seen some slow queues outside the Town ground, but this one's taking the biscuit.

'Have they opened the gates yet?' I enquire of a passing steward, only slightly sarcastically.

'Yes, but they've had to close them again for health and safety reasons,' she replies.

'Health and safety reasons?' I ask, bemused. Surely Town can cope with a moderately large crowd.

'Yes. Half the lights have gone off in the ground, and we can't let anyone in until they're back on.'

'Oh,' is all I can reply as the penny drops.

We have nothing to do, but wait. It starts to rain and there's still no sign of light or movement. The owners of The Woodlands pub down the road must be rubbing their hands together in glee as some Town fans join Portsmouth fans for an extra hour of drinking. I'd like to join them, but we need to get in once the gates open and grab a good space on the barriers.

Then, another first for Harrogate Town: a man walks down the long, wet line selling, wait for it, half-and-half Harrogate-Portsmouth scarves. Now, I've never seen the point of buying half and half scarves myself. Why would you want to wear the colours of your opponent, and why on earth would you want to buy a scarf that can only be worn once? I can just about understand half and half badges, as people like to collect badges. But my understanding only stretches as far as the match being The FA Cup Final itself.

Eventually, after forty five minutes of standing in the rain, someone somewhere finds the right plug and the stadium lights flicker on, to cheers. Then they go off again, to groans. Thankfully, the second power outage is short-lived, and more cheers are soon heard from the direction of the turnstiles as the queue starts to move.

We're in for 7.45, but the match is delayed by an hour, to allow everyone time to get in, Woodlands pub clientele included. There's another scare as the lights go out again twenty minutes before kick-off, and the crowd turns into a sea of lit up smart phones. *'We're Harrogate Town, we'll play in the dark,'* sings the Kop. Somehow, I don't think BT Sport viewers will approve. I show my age by telling Molly's friends that when the floodlights went out back in the day, people used to hold up lit matches.

When the teams eventually kick off, we've already been waiting for a period as long as the match itself, and that includes the half-time period. We learn later that we came within minutes, or one more power failure, of the referee abandoning the match altogether.

The wait's worth it though, as Town are quick out of the blocks, dictating play and stretching our League One opponents. A good start turns into a dream start as Beck heads us deservedly in front. The players are up for it alright, not giving Portsmouth a chance to settle on the ball, and Beck is winning absolutely everything in the air, creating havoc, as the visitors look surprisingly open at the back.

Dreamland lasts for ten minutes longer, before the visiting full back, Haunstrup, cuts inside across the Town area, unleashing an unstoppable curling shot past Belshaw. The second goal is even better, a thirty yard stunner from Curtis that leaves Belshaw clutching at thin air. I could be hard on Town for not closing him down, but it's just a wonder strike. The irony is that Burrell had been snuffing out danger in that area of the pitch brilliantly until he'd been forced to withdraw through injury on the half hour mark. Thankfully he managed to walk off safely and avoid smashing his head on the top of the dugout, unlike the unlucky visiting defender who limped off injured early in the match.

That confounded Portsmouth bell suddenly gets very annoying and I'm glad I don't have to listen to it every week. The Town drum, allowed in tonight under equal opportunities, has gone quiet. It's hard on Town, but heads don't drop. Falkingham and Emmett keep pressing and passing and mixing it up with long balls on to the head of Beck, but Portsmouth have tightened up in the second half, winning more possession and coming very close a couple of times at the other end.

Urged on by the crowd, Town push hard for an equaliser in the final fifteen minutes, but Pompey hold firm, restricting us to a couple of half chances for Beck and a Thomson long range strike, as Town dictate play and try to pass through the visiting defence. And that's the sole difference between the teams tonight; the visitors' clinical finishing versus Town's hesitancy, or inability to get a shot away, or lash a dangerous cross into the area, albeit against a capable League One defence.

There'll be no home tie against Altrincham in the Second Round, but I couldn't be prouder of this team, going toe-to-toe with our illustrious opponents and looking every bit as accomplished. It's another mark of our incredible progress that we're disappointed with not managing at least a draw tonight. If Town can replicate this form in the league, whilst adding goals, it's going to be one hell of a ride.

Walking out of the ground, with the clock ticking on for eleven, I can even feel a little sympathy for the Pompey fans, bell and all, facing a long, wet, overnight journey home to the south coast.

One very proud dad kicks a man whilst he's down. Meanwhile, Town let a three goal lead slip

Bromley (A) D 3-3. Goals: Emmett, Kiernan, Muldoon. Crowd: 2,177. Article originally published on Thursday 21st November 2019 under the title *'Bromley clash was a rollercoaster of emotions packed into ninety minutes.'*

Last week happened in such a blur that I barely had two hours to write and submit my column on the Portsmouth Cup tie. Now, having had time to muse on things a little bit more, here's a couple of further thoughts.

It was a fantastic sight to see a packed crowd creating a football league-type atmosphere inside the ground, but one thing had been puzzling me all week. The fixture was announced as completely sold out prior to kick off, with the crowd announced as 3,042 over the tannoy. Yet something didn't seem right, and there was an audible disappointment in the Kop when it was announced, as our official capacity is 4,000. Even taking into account the very small 'no man's land' in the Wetherby Road stand and the area cordoned off for the BT Sport cameras, I was wondering what had happened to the missing few hundred. Two years ago, 2,800 had crammed happily into the ground, when York were the visitors, and this was before the three new stands we have now were even built. Well now the mystery has been solved. It turns out that the crowd figure was actually announced wrongly over the PA and the official figure was a very healthy 3,402.

I think we can all agree that Mark Beck had a great match, but one of the reasons I think he had so much joy in the aerial battles was due to the lack of shirt holding and arm wrestling from the Portsmouth defence. It was something that was really refreshing to witness, having seen so much of it week in week out in the National League. An early push in the back on our big target man was penalised by the referee and I wonder whether this contributed to the way he was treated. Even so, Portsmouth played it fair and in good spirit throughout. It was also a pleasant change to witness a decent referee in full control of the game, as opposed to some of the shocking officials we've seen down at Wetherby Road in recent times. The National League really needs to start clamping down on shirt pulling, but I won't hold my breath.

Although Town may have been eliminated from the Cup, I do have news of success for another Harrogate team last week. St. Aidan's U16 girls' team, complete with Molly in defence, made the short trip to Tadcaster Grammar and came away with a victory in the first round of their own cup competition. The match finished 0-0 after extra time, before St. Aidan's came out on top in a tense penalty shoot-out by 5 goals to 4. Molly took a ball in the face, but completed most of the match despite bleeding from a badly swollen lip, helping her team to that valuable clean sheet in the process. Needless to say, I'm one very proud dad at the moment.

Moving on to this week, it's fair to say that I would have taken a draw at Bromley prior to the match on Saturday. But am I happy? Well, yes and no.

I found myself in town, Christmas shopping, during the first half and couldn't prevent myself from cheering in the Victoria Shopping Centre when Emmett put us 1-0 up on Twitter. It's then that my internet signal went down. I managed to arrive back at the car in time to hear Bromley equalise just before half-time on Radio York, or so I thought. Imagine my shock when the commentator announced the score as 3-1 to Town.

On reaching home, Molly ran out excitedly to the car with a tube of Pringles and a tin of sweets, and we settled down in the heated front seats to listen to the second half, both hopeful of a Town win. It didn't pan out like that, of course, as the home team threw everything but the kitchen sink at us, and our emotions ran the complete gauntlet from happy to hopeful to anxious to utterly depressed to outright relieved that we'd managed to salvage a point out of three at the league leaders' expense.

Following this self-inflicted torture, I headed off into Leeds where I was working overnight on Moortown Roundabout.

'Your team let me down badly today,' said one of the surfacing contractors on my arrival.

I wasn't expecting that, so I asked him why. It turns out that he'd put an accumulator bet on the outcome of six matches earlier and the Town result was the only one that had stood between himself and a large payout. I started apologising for the fact that Town let a three goal lead slip.

'Oh no,' he clarified, *'I had Bromley down to win.'*

Well, what on earth could I say to that? I could have been empathetic, but no, I found myself replying, *'Did you know that Bromley hit the crossbar in injury time?'* Of course he didn't.

Talk about kicking a man while he's down.

A Fallowfield wonder goal, two comedy own goals and a death stare

Chesterfield (H) W 3-1. Goals: Falkingham, Fallowfield, Muldoon. Crowd: 1,710. FC Halifax Town (H) D 2-2. Goals: o.g. 2. Crowd: 1,185. Article originally published on Thursday 28th November 2019 under the title *'Taking on Chesterfield and Halifax as favourites – who'd have thought it?'*

I've been looking forward to this week for some time, with fallen 'giants' Chesterfield and Halifax both in town in the space of four days. When Molly and I started attending matches five seasons ago, little did I think I'd be writing a sentence like that and treating it as almost routine, never mind the fact it could be argued that Town enter both matches as favourites.

Chesterfield on the Saturday is one of those matches you live for. There's a decent crowd, a boisterous away following and Town kick off with a high intensity, looking as if they mean business against a team flirting with relegation. Football rarely goes to plan though, and Chesterfield hit us with a breakaway goal ten minutes in, before stretching Belshaw twice, as the match turns in the visitors' favour.

Town rally as the half wears on, successfully mixing up their passing game with longer balls to the head of a Mark Beck who can currently do no wrong. Nearly every ball that he knocks on causes danger and it's from this route that Falkingham equalises.

It's a six minute spell in the second half though that will stick long in the memory. First, Thomson nicks the ball in midfield and slides it into the path of Fallowfield, approaching with the velocity of an intercity train though the mist. *'Shoot!'* shouts the Kop in unison, as he smashes a swerving rocket of a shot into the top right hand corner of the net, before tearing away to the new 'Meccano' Stand to celebrate. He later admits on my daughter's Instagram feed that he'd aimed for the opposite corner, but I'm not going to let that spoil the moment. Is there a better attacking full back in the league at the moment than Fallowfield?

Two minutes later, Beck turns and cracks a long range scorcher towards goal. The flailing keeper does well to keep it out but can only parry it back into the path of an on-rushing Muldoon who, unbelievably, lifts it over the bar. I look at Molly. She has her head in her hands in disbelief, but the visitors are rocking as Town hit a purple patch. Minutes later, Thomson slides the ball through to an undeterred Muldoon, who finds himself one-on-one with the keeper. With Thomson running through on his right for a tap in, and me screaming *'square it!'*, Muldoon chooses to take the ball round the unfortunate stopper and slide it in himself.

Mitch Hancox, our new left back from Solihull, completes a solid debut. Although the early Chesterfield goal comes from his flank, as he struggles early on against the pacey McGlashan, he grows into the game as Chesterfield fade, whilst delivering a number of dangerous corners and free-kicks. If I have one criticism of Town in recent weeks, it's that the quality of our dead-ball delivery into the opposition box has been poor. I've often wondered whether we could get Joe Leesley back from Stockport and bring him off the bench at dead-ball situations, just like those old Subbuteo corner kickers. It seems, however, that the addition of Hancox may be a shrewd move in this respect.

Although we're unbeaten in four at the Shay and Halifax are currently on a bad run that sees them third from bottom in the recent form table, Tuesday night could well turn out to be a potential banana skin, as the Shaymen always seem to raise their game at our place. And so it proves.

The weekly Non-League Paper described Town as 'relentless' against Chesterfield, but tonight's first half performance on a soggy, uninspiring evening, could be described as more listless than relentless. Like the weather, Town seem slightly off the pace, going in 1-0 down at the break to a McAlinden penalty. Nothing, though, can prepare us for the bizarre nature of the second half.

Town take the game to the visitors but just can't put the ball into the net, until an unfortunate Brown slides the ball past his own keeper from a low cross, with Beck lurking. The goal's initially credited to Thomson, but it's a definite own goal.

The game's there for Town's taking, but it's our opponents who hold firm before mugging us on the break twelve minutes from time. Then, as the match edges towards the last five minutes, Burrell tries to routinely control a high ball in midfield. No one gives it a second thought until the referee blows up and brandishes a straight red card for dangerous play. A disbelieving Burrell disappears down the tunnel in front of us. It's another absolute shocker of a sending off from a poor National League referee. That's it, game over. Or so we think.

Ten man Town valiantly take the game to Halifax, coming close a couple of times, before, in injury time, another low cross is sliced into his own net in similar, but much more farcical fashion, by Staunton. Unbridled joy breaks out in the 1919 end. I don't know whether to laugh or celebrate. Molly sings *'Who put the ball in the Shaymen's net? Half the Halifax team did!'* A slight exaggeration, I know, but you get the drift. Four goals, and not one of them scored by a Town player.

The unhappy Halifax players trudge off the field at the end past the celebrating Town fans. The captain, Brown, gives us an absolute death stare as we wave cheerily back to him.

So, after all that excitement, the week ends more or less as it began, with Town nestling in the play-off positions, just four points off the top. I'm trying not to get my hopes up, but when do I start referring to Town as genuine promotion contenders?

Bigmouth strikes again

Sutton United (A) L 1-3. Goal: Falkingham. Crowd: 1,490. Article originally published on Thursday 5th December 2019 under the title *'Pleasantly surprised by Town's league position at halfway stage of 2019/20.'*

Well that will teach me to open my big mouth.

Signing off this column, as I did last week, with the word *'Town'* nestling next to *'serious promotion contenders'* didn't even survive the scrutiny of a week. The loss at fifth from bottom Sutton United, a team with only one win at home in the league prior to Saturday, saw Town suffer defeat for only the second time in fifteen league games. From now on, I'm keeping my big mouth firmly shut.

Although one player doesn't make a team, Warren Burrell was sorely missed at Gander Green Lane. The FA's rejection of Town's appeal against his shocking and unjust red card against Halifax, for nothing more than attempting to control the ball in midfield, beggars belief and just piles insult on to injury. Not that we're struggling for central midfield replacements though, with Emmett, Bradley and a fit again Kerry all vying for a starting place alongside Falkingham.

As we now find ourselves one game past the halfway point of the season, having played everyone at least once, Hartlepool excepted, I thought it would be a good time to pause and reflect.

Last season I wrote that if we wanted to challenge for the title, we'd have to break through the glass ceiling of winning against the sides around us, as we came out distinctly second best against promotion rivals Leyton Orient, Salford, Wrexham, Solihull and Fylde.

This year has been the polar opposite, with Town winning at promotion rivals Halifax, Yeovil and Barrow, drawing at Bromley and at home to Solihull and Halifax. The only loss to a top seven side coming early in the season at Woking, when the home team lucked a cruel, wind-assisted goal, totally against the run of play. The advantage for Town, moving forward, is that the only away trip left to a current top six side is the visit to Solihull.

You'd have thought that, based on the performances against the teams around us, Town would be closer to the top than they actually are, but therein lies the problem. A series of disappointing defeats away from home at southern-based Dagenham, Sutton, Torquay and Eastleigh have let the side down, and it's this problem of consistency that Town need to address if they wish to seriously challenge for the title. The gritty, dogged display shown, for example, at Yeovil needs to be replicated more often on the road.

Taking into account the loss of Callum Howe in the week before the big kick-off and the indifferent start, I'm happy to state that I'm pleasantly surprised with the current position in the table, sitting in the thick of the play-off race, seven points off top. Looking on the cautious side, five more wins should see us retain our place in the National League for another year. Now we just need to avoid the almost customary Christmas slump in form.

Who'd have thought though, at this stage, that we'd be looking at Wrexham propping up the table and Barrow sitting proudly on top of the pile, especially after our demolition of the Cumbrians at Holker Street, two matches in.

If Town are to maintain a challenge, however, I feel that Simon Weaver needs to bring in another striker, preferably someone young, hungry and with a goal threat. The loaning out of Jones to Solihull makes this even more of a priority. In light of the fact that we signed a Brown, Smith, Smith, Jones, Hall and Stead in the close season, seemingly making an attempt for the record number of most common British surnames in one team, maybe we could sign a Williams at centre forward.

Ah, wait a minute...

Sick of being sick.
A weird sense
of deja vu

Torquay United (H) W 2-1. Goals: Bradley, Stead. Crowd: 1,348.
Article originally published on Thursday 12th December 2019 under
the title *'It wouldn't be a true Town experience without having to
endure a nervy finale.'*

Regular readers of this column may recall that I slept
through the Torquay away fixture earlier in the season,
following a bout of severe sickness on the Stray. Well, this
Saturday sees me in bed again with a less severe bout of man
flu, drifting in and out of sleep...

'Dad... Dad...'

'Wha...?'

'Dad. I'm off to meet Lily,' shouts Molly. *'Are you not going
to the match?'*

'Er, what time is it?' My eyes focus on the clock, it's twenty
to three. How on earth did that happen?

'You go, I'll see you at the ground,' I say, hurriedly jumping
out of bed. What is it about Torquay and sleep?

There's no time to make my customary flask of coffee as I
dash around looking for my season ticket, scarf, hat and coat.
The good thing is we live really close, so I'm in the ground
just before kick-off. Molly and Lily are already in the Kop.

As far as I'm concerned, we owe today's visitors for the
heavy defeat they inflicted on us down in Devon. Now's the

time to play them, as they've lost four on the bounce and conceded five at home to Stockport last week.

It's a slow start but Town open the scoring early and manage to solve a personal mystery. I've previously wondered aloud in this column why all the players crush over to one side of the pitch when the keeper takes a goal kick. I've often thought, why doesn't our fastest player just peel off to the right at the last minute to receive a pass from Belshaw? He'd be completely through on goal, unopposed. It never happens though, until today. Well, sort of.

Belshaw duly kicks into the scrum, the ball breaks to Thomson in central midfield and he picks out temporary right back, Bradley, racing down the right flank all on his own. It's a carbon copy of the Fallowfield scorcher the other week. Well it may have been, if Bradley had listened to the Kop and hit it first time. Instead he chooses to cut in left, past two defenders chasing back, before tickling a weak shot towards goal. The keeper stifles a yawn and kneels down to collect the ball, but it takes a deflection off a defender's boot and zips past him into the net. It's comedy central, but we don't care, as the keeper holds his head in his hands before going berserk at the unfortunate defender. That's three home goals in a row now all involving heavy deflections. It's nice to see our luck turning.

And that's about it for the first half, save for a rasping Muldoon effort right on half-time. The visitors have seen a lot of possession in between, and don't look like a team lacking in confidence. Town seem to have forgotten how to pass the ball in midfield, and also seem to have forgotten that Beck isn't in the team, as they keep lumping it forward under pressure. I'm assured by at least two fans that they were much worse last week at Sutton, so I'll take the lead thank you.

Not for the first time this season, Town come out all guns blazing for the first twenty minutes of the second half. The manager's obviously told them to press high and pass the ball a bit more. The second goal, when it arrives is another instance of deja vu, but there's no lucky deflection here.

Kiernan and Hancox combine to good effect down the left, and Jon Stead, making only his fifth start, uses all his experience to hang back near the penalty spot and direct the low cross into the top of the net. It's Stead's third of the season, the other two being against, yes you guessed it, Torquay in the aforementioned away fixture.

You'd think this would be game over against a fragile visiting side, but it wouldn't be Town without the home fans having to endure an edgy last twenty minutes following a Torquay penalty.

See it out the players do though, in front of another encouraging attendance of 1,348, swelled by an impressive away following in the high two hundreds. I could be wrong, but I seem to recall seeing Torquay followings back in the mists of time numbering in the low double figures. There's certainly life outside the Football League. The one thing that stands out for me today though, is the healthy number of under-sixteens in attendance at the front of the Kop. Has the welcome reduction back down to £5 helped in this regard?

It's the Supporter's Club Christmas party straight after the match in the 1919 and I'd love to go, have a drink and meet the players. Molly wants to win the signed shirt, but we make our excuses and head for home. I'd like to say that the reason we didn't go was because I was wary of passing my germs on to the players, but I'm afraid I'd be lying. You see I'd promised we'd go to Ikea to pick up a Christmas tree, once I was feeling better, and I didn't think it would be a good move to return home late and incapable of driving, having looked at a pint of lager. Oh well, there's always next year.

'We all know Hartlepool have a habit of shooting themselves in the foot, but this was something else. They got out their 12 gauge shotgun and left themselves without a leg to stand on'
(The Hartlepool Mail)

Hartlepool United (H) (FA Trophy First Round) W 3-2. Goals: o.g., Hall, Kiernan. Crowd: 803. Article originally published on Thursday 19th December 2019 under the title *'Late fight back shows exactly why you should never, ever leave a match early'*

'Can we actually leave early?' asks Molly twenty minutes into the second half of what, so far, has been the most abject of Town FA Trophy performances. We're two down to visitors Hartlepool and, despite a slightly better second half effort, now that Brown and Emmett are on, Town aren't showing many convincing signs of being able to pull the deficit back. To further compound the misery, horizontal sheets of freezing rain are lashing across the ground, in the sort of weather not seen since last season, when York City were the visitors in the same competition.

I'm a little taken aback. She's never ever wanted to leave a match early since we started attending, and I'm not sure whether she's entirely serious. I did say I wanted to stay in the bar at half-time, rather than emerge for the second half, but that's just me. I don't expect such defeatism from my daughter.

'*They may not let us out. We could be locked in,*' I reply, thinking that would explain why nobody's left so far. What I don't tell her is that I've never left a match early in all my years of watching football, and I'm certainly not going to start now. No matter how bad it is on the pitch for my team, I just can't up sticks and leave them to carry on. After all, you wouldn't pay to watch a film and leave before the end now, would you?

'*You can go if you want,*' I say to my daughter and her friends but, bluff duly called, stay they do. Maybe she wasn't serious after all. It's just then that one of the home and away regulars decides to head off to the bar to drown his sorrows. I'm thinking maybe this was the match to miss in order to finish the Christmas shopping, as many other home fans appear to have done.

The Hartlepool keeper, Dimi Kontstantopoulos, is a club legend, who, at 41 years old, is making his second debut fifteen years after the first. He hasn't put a foot wrong so far, even saving a Stead penalty. The away end is singing his name and I sadly announce to the fan next to me that I can't see how Town are going to put three goals past him tonight. Well, what do I know?

With thirteen minutes to go, the visitors decide to give us a helping hand. A low, hopeful Hancox cross loops up high off a Pools' defender and over the keeper into the net; continuing the freakish run of visiting own goals at Wetherby Road. We cheer more in consolation than expectation. Even so, it's undoubtedly game on.

For those of you in a hurry, wishing to leave this column now, I'll quote the Hartlepool Mail again. *'Pools now had to hold on to their slender advantage for the final thirteen minutes of the match. Could they do that? Of course not.'*

Just four minutes from the end, the keeper jumps up to catch a routine, loose high ball. Under pressure from Connor Hall, he sheds the ball at our central defender's feet and suddenly it's two each. I don't know whether to celebrate, as I'm convinced the hitherto picky referee is going to disallow the goal for a nudge on the keeper. I can only presume this is what most goal celebrations feel like in the Premier League following the introduction of VAR. Kontstantopoulos makes a meal of having being caught in the ribs and goes down for lengthy treatment, but the referee's having none of it, pointing to the centre circle to indicate a goal. Yes!!

We're deep into injury time, heading into extra time, when lightning unbelievably strikes twice. A hapless visiting defender slices the ball high backwards into the air. The reinvigorated Town end shouts *'whoooah'* as the spinning ball spirals down towards the unfortunate keeper. He closes his eyes, holds out his hands hopefully and the by now, greasy ball slides through his grasp under token pressure from Emmett, and straight into the path of Kiernan who passes it from six yards into the gaping empty net. My eyes dart to the referee again. Goal!!! The Town fans and players celebrate wildly, whilst a mass exodus begins in the away end. I know what I said earlier about leaving early, but I'd have been contemplating the same myself if I was one of them.

The five hundred or so of us home fans in attendance, and not in the bar, on this bitterly cold pre-Christmas afternoon will long cherish today as one of the most bizarre turnarounds we've ever witnessed. It's not so much a glorious comeback, more an epic tale of self-destruction by the visitors. We're through the looking glass into a land where logic is reversed. When the *'How To Defend A Two Goal Lead For Dummies'* manual is written, this game will feature as a prime example of how not to do it. Not that anyone in yellow and black cares one iota.

Death or Chorley

Boreham Wood (A) L 1-2. Goal: Bradley. Crowd: 501. Hartlepool United (H) W 4-1. Goals: Kerry, Muldoon 2, Falkingham. Crowd: 2,383. Chorley (A) W 2-0. Goals: Muldoon, Stead. Crowd: 1,077. Article originally published on Thursday 2nd January 2020 under the title *'No complaints after trip across the Pennines to a proper football ground.'*

Although it's deja vu in the sense that we're playing Hartlepool at home for the second time in thirteen days, this Boxing Day fixture sees a threefold increase in the attendance from the previous Trophy encounter, with almost 2,400 inside the ground, boosted by over 900 from the North East. It's a cracking atmosphere, with the visiting fans certainly up for it. Boxing Day and football are simply just made for each other.

The first half fails to live up to the atmosphere off the pitch however, as both teams conspire to cancel each other out. Town have a lot of possession but fall into the frustrating trap of passing sideways and backwards, inviting the visitors to push high. It's a marked improvement on our first half showing last time out though, so I'll take the positives.

The manager must have seen what I've seen, because Town come out like a team possessed in the second half, as do the hitherto slightly subdued Town fans. We're now reunited in the Kop end, after being split in two minds between the 1919 and Kop ends during the first half, and the early minutes resemble a sing-off between the two sets of supporters.

The Town passing is sharp, incisive and to forward running players, as a vulnerable Hartlepool are sliced open three times in the space of fifteen minutes. It's fair to say that Jon Stead has had a difficult start to his Town career, but he now seems to be finding his feet, assisting both the first two goals, albeit letting Muldoon take the penalty for the second of the two, having been pushed over in the area.

The visitors eventually manage to pull one back and then press hard for a second, piling up for a corner in the 91st minute. The ball breaks to Muldoon on the edge of the Town area, he side steps a couple of defenders, sees a gap and he's away like a greyhound out of the trap. Visiting defenders fall over trying to block Emmett in the centre circle, but they've got the wrong man. In the blink of an eye, Muldoon's past them all unchallenged and heading towards us, in on goal, hapless defenders trailing in his wake. He's so fast, he has time to think before executing the most delicious of chips over the advancing keeper and into the net. It's a goal worthy of the Premier League, although I think the *Match Of The Day* pundits may have something to say about the National League North-standard defending.

For the second time in thirteen days, a mass exodus of Hartlepool fans ensues. Their team really don't deserve the support they've been getting.

Fast forward forty eight hours, and I've been looking forward to the short trip across the Pennines to Chorley for a while now. I've visited many grounds across the North, but never Victory Park, until today. It doesn't disappoint.

Nestling off the main road adjacent to a park and in amongst rows of terraced houses, the coach drops us off as close to the ground as we can get, an hour before kick-off.

Molly's first impressions are that *'it's a bit of a dump'* and, while I can see her point, I have to admit that's exactly what I like about it. It's a proper northern football ground from the days when we used to be in the National League North (oh how good it feels to say that).

We hit the clubhouse to get some warmth and sustenance and then settle in a shallow terraced, huge shed behind one goal that has all the look and feel of a 1970's bus depot.

Town, of course, elect to kick the other way, so the sizeable and noisy away support moves round to a smaller and cosier shed, perched on the bank opposite, decorated with painted murals to the glory of Chorley FC, although some spoilsport has attempted to scrawl 'SCFC' in marker pen across them.

There's an unkempt grass bank along the side of the pitch to the right of us, with a tiny temporary stand perched high on the halfway line and a large Football League-size, old-fashioned seated stand, with terraced paddock in front, to the left of us. Molly's right, the ground has seen better days, but it makes a pleasant change from banks of sterile, empty blue plastic seats at Halifax and Chesterfield.

The first half, much like Boxing Day against Hartlepool, is a bit of a stalemate. The difference here is that Town take their one real chance in clinical fashion, an on-fire Muldoon racing through to hammer low into the corner decisively past the keeper. Chorley, as expected, are rugged and up for it, but lack quality where it matters.

The second half finds us safely nestled back in the bus depot end, with the Chorley support having moved en masse to the end we've just vacated. Town step up a gear after half-time, again like Boxing Day, and really should be three or four up before Stead once more exploits Chorley's weakness by getting in behind them and slotting in from a narrow angle.

'*Staying up, stay-ing up!*' chant the Town fans, cautiously yet joyously, and just maybe a little sarcastically. Chorley will remain rooted to the bottom tonight, but I wish them well.

Even then, there's time for Town to squander another couple of gilt-edged chances, but it's a job well done.

Before the match, away travel organiser Jordan Ford informs us that Chorley have requested that the coach stays back for a while after the final whistle, so as not to add to congestion outside the ground. It's a bizarre request and leads to a bit of head scratching on the coach. Now it all makes sense, as it gives us 45 minutes to drink in the clubhouse again. I'm not saying that Jordan made it up, no I'm not saying that at all, but when we eventually set off back for Yorkshire, a little the worse for wear, there's not a vehicle in sight, and there hasn't been for at least the last twenty minutes.

Not that anyone is complaining, as we wend our way back home past the dark Pendle hills with Town sitting nicely three points off top, and all three teams above them yet to visit Wetherby Road.

Keep on keepin' on.
One nil to
the Harrogate.

Hartlepool United (A) W 1-0. Goal: Stead. Crowd: 3,481. Maidenhead United (H) W 1-0. Goal: Hall. Crowd: 1,281. Article originally published on Thursday 9th January 2020 under the title *'Harrogate haven't looked back since our first visit to Hartlepool last season.'*

Our first ever visit to Hartlepool last season was truly a journey into the unknown. Town had just achieved National League status for the first time in their history and this was our first away trip in the big league on the Tuesday night. It seemed a tough place to go. How would we fare? Were we in for a season of consolidation or struggle? As it turned out, we played some great football that night, came away buoyant with a two-all draw, and haven't looked back since.

This New Year's Day, Molly and I are heading back to Hartlepool on the later of two coaches, and she's reminding me of the match last season when Hartlepool scored and she laughed out loud. Not because she was particularly happy at Town conceding, but because the PA system broke out into a loud rendition of The Piranhas' *'Tom Hark'* in celebration. Me, I scowled. I hate that kind of fake celebration. Just don't get me started on those huge flags that unfurl behind the goals at the Emirates every time Arsenal score.

When I visited Hartlepool's ground in the late eighties, the adjacent docks were fairly run down. I spent a happy half hour wandering round what seemed like a huge scrap yard, gawping at all the rusty ships. Now it's turned into a new Marina behind a brick wall, with an adjacent retail park, so with a full hour to kill outside the ground, we head off to find the earlier coach-load of Town supporters in the Raglan Quoit Club just up the road.

The Raglan's a fairly run-down, unassuming building with a smoking shelter outside. We pass the vaping Hartlepool fans and poke our noses round the door of what looks like a back entrance. There are just a few home fans inside. So I decide to drag Molly to the pub on the edge of town where we went last season. It's just home fans there too.

'Your lot are in the Raglan Quoit,' a passing fan who's just left the club informs me.

'But we've just been there,' I protest, not quite believing him.

Nonetheless, we head off back to the Raglan and, lo and behold, there's another previously undiscovered cosy bar with four television screens showing two live Premier League matches, pool and snooker tables, a coach load of Town fans and a smattering of Hartlepool fans. It's the ultimate Tardis experience. I order a pint of Trophy and half a lemonade from the friendly bar staff, part with a tenner and receive £7.70 in change. I think I've just died and gone to heaven. I get chatting to a Geordie, and it turns out that we were at the same Newcastle v Wolves match in 1990, when the Midlanders broke the record for the most fans travelling to a domestic league match by air, although I bucked the trend and went in the car.

After the friendly welcome in the Raglan Quoit, and

having watched Brighton peg back Chelsea on TV, it all goes downhill at the ground. Chief Brody, our local blogging superstar, has been told he's not allowed to film in the ground *'without a licence.'* Furthermore, the drum has been refused entry. It's not a good look.

I then conspire to miss much of the first twenty minutes of the match whilst trying to obtain a portion of chips from the refreshment kiosk. If the sole assistant is not taking an inordinate amount of time to deep fry them, she's busy selling the three portions she's just cooked to the person who sneaked in front of me, whilst I snuck back to take a peep at the match. Finally, when I'm at the kiosk and there's actually a portion of chips waiting for me, the lone assistant decides to slowly count out a huge cash float first, before serving me.

It turns out I haven't missed much as both teams again cancel each other out for much of the first half. The chips are worth the wait though.

With chances at a premium, Town make the second half breakthrough. A brilliant piece of footwork by Bradley puts Emmett in behind the Hartlepool defence and Stead is there in the six yard box to steer in the resultant cross, despite the best attempts of a home defender to pull him back. Emmett has done well to get this far, playing the match with a black eye, even before being taken out on the half way line a few minutes earlier, by the hardest tackle I've ever witnessed in a football match. It was like he ran into a solid brick wall, and I couldn't see him getting up and continuing. Thankfully, he did.

The home team huff and puff, looking slightly better than in their two recent defeats at Wetherby Road, but Town manage to hold on to the lead without any major scares. *'Tom Hark'* will not be aired today. The percussion-less Town end celebrates wildly at the final whistle.

The visit of Maidenhead on the following Saturday should be a nailed on home win if the table is to be believed, but Town struggle to create chances against a well-drilled visiting team in front of the second most pointlessly segregated crowd this season.

Not only are the 42 Maidenhead fans fenced off, but there's a 'no man's land' in the Town end. I understand the need for segregation when 900 Hartlepool fans are in town, but reinstating the freedom of the ground for all fans on days like today would have a number of distinct advantages. Town fans would be able to congregate in the Wetherby Road stand again and cheer the team on when attacking the 1919 end, the overall bar and club shop take would be up, the biggest refreshment kiosk in the ground would again do a brisk trade, and away fans would have a better day out.

Meanwhile back on the pitch, the visiting centre half, Ellul, is winning everything pumped up to Stead and, if he can't win it fairly, an arm in the nape of Stead's neck, on the blindside of the referee, does the job. We cheer as we win a corner at the 1919 end, but it's so obvious that it's going to Hall at the back post again, that it's snuffed out by three defenders.

Town need three points to stay in touch with Barrow, who are thrashing Ebbsfleet, but it looks like this match could turn out to be one of those giant banana skins we seem to encounter every now and again. *'I'll take a scrappy one-nil,'* a passing Town fans tells me at half-time. And that's exactly what we eventually get.

Fifteen minutes into the second period, we again cheer for a corner, although I don't know why, as nothing's come of them so far. *'Try something different,'* I plead internally, as Bradley lines up to take it. He hoists it towards the back post again, but this time Hall's lost the entire visiting defence. His volley into the six yard box cannons off an unfortunate defender and in. Hall shouts in delight, wheels away and high-fives me in the crowd as he passes.

Town barely venture down our end again for the remainder of the second half, but manage to successfully shut the door at the other end for the third game in a row, helped not inconsiderably by the visitors losing their heads and seeing red twice in five self-destructive minutes.

We've seen two games in four days, both decided by the finest of margins, and Town are turning into serious promotion contenders. The only problem appears to be that Barrow keep on winning but, as Simon Weaver so succinctly put it on Radio York, they must be looking at the teams below and thinking, *'What on earth do we have to do to shake them off?'*

Dad, you'll just have to wait. I'm off up to Darlington

Darlington (A) (FA Trophy Second Round) W 2-0. Goals: Diamond, Kerry. Crowd: 1,240. Article originally published on Thursday 16th January 2020 under the title *'Much-changed side's win over Quakers demonstrates Town's strength in depth.'*

I'd originally planned to travel down to the West Midlands to visit my dad this weekend. I'm ashamed to say, though, that there was an ulterior motive involved. My plans abruptly changed when Darlington unexpectedly knocked Solihull Moors out of the FA Trophy in midweek.

As usual, my wife hits the nail on the head. *'Have you decided not to go to your dad's because you want to go to Darlington?'*

'Well it was a bit short notice for him,' I offer in response, but yes, she's right and she knows it. She hasn't twigged about the original Solihull plan though.

Come the Saturday and my wife and I are tootling up to Darlington via a short stop off in busy Northallerton. It's free parking for the first half an hour, so it's a win-win.

On arrival in Darlington, I leave my wife in the town centre, agreeing to meet her at a quarter past five, before setting off on the twenty minute walk to the ground. Molly's back in Harrogate at a party today, so I'm Billy-No-Mates.

In a very unofficial poll of Town fans' least favourite grounds to visit on Facebook, I'm pretty sure Darlington's ground came out on top. It's not segregated as such when

Town visit, but the popular 1,000 capacity Tin Shed End behind one goal is not somewhere visiting fans would be allowed to congregate. The 'away' end is nothing more than a pathed walkway in front of a small grass bank. There's no terracing or cover if it rains and no atmosphere, whatever the weather. There are plans to build a stand on the away end and to improve the ground further, but it all depends on the fans being able to raise enough cash.

However, the fact that Darlington are here at all is a minor miracle. In 2011-12 the club was placed into administration for the third time in ten years and eventually expelled from the league after failing to pay its debts. A new fan/community owned club, Darlington 1883, started life the following season in the Northern League First Division, alongside Newton Aycliffe, Bedlington Terriers and Norton & Stockton Ancients, at Level 9 of the football pyramid, playing their football at Bishop Auckland's ground. I was present at a league match at Station View as recently as 2014 when Darlington were the visitors to Harrogate Railway in a fetching pink strip. Three promotions in four years saw them in the National League North, and in 2016 the club secured a move back to Darlington to play football at the rugby ground, Blackwell Meadows, out on the edge of town.

There's a fair smattering of Town fans today to see a rotated squad, minus Belshaw, Falkingham, Emmett, Stead, Hall and Muldoon. Here's the thing though. You couldn't call this a weakened team by any stretch of the imagination, as the outfield replacements (Beck, Thomson, Kiernan and Fallowfield) are all bona fida first team regulars and all unlucky to be out of the current team. Our latest left back loanee, Owen Gallacher, makes his senior debut and Cracknell makes a rare appearance in goal.

Although we have a small squad, it's a tight, close knit bunch of players. Everyone has a contribution to make, and there's no weak link. I have my favourites, of course, but I'm happy for any of these players to start, and today just reinforces that opinion.

The two current full backs, Bradley and Burrell, are moved effortlessly back into central midfield, a position they're both comfortable with. It's all a testament to Simon Weaver's shrewd recruitment.

The most heartening thing is that Town actually look like a team a league above their opponents, passing the ball around slickly and looking dangerous once they hit their stride in the first half. Jack Diamond has been lively since he arrived, but if I have one very minor criticism it's that his end product in terms of goals and assists has been lacking. Not today. His opening goal is sharp, clinical and coolly taken and he comes close to doubling his tally a couple of minutes later with a vicious, swerving twenty-five yarder that the keeper does well to tip over.

There's drama at half-time as a group of young Darlington fans run past us in the food queue with one of the Town banners that they've liberated from the 'away' end, but all's well and good as it's eventually retrieved. Maybe they ought to make one of their own, as ours is the wrong colour.

Town really should be two or three up, having hit the woodwork twice and coming close on a number of other occasions, as Darlington eventually work up a head of steam in the last fifteen minutes. It's looking slightly dicey as we're pushed further back and the home team start to create chances. I'm standing next to a home fan and he tells me that this is when Darlington are at their most dangerous, having scored a number of late goals.

The home fans, and fan to the left of me, scream for a foul as one of their players tumbles to the ground under minimal contact. *'That's never a foul, it's a contact sport,'* I say very loudly. Moments later, Kiernan goes down under a challenge in the area. Town fans scream for a penalty. I'm not sure from where I'm standing, I'd need to see VAR. *'I thought it was a contact sport,'* says a voice to the left of me. He then proceeds to take his frustrations out on the advertising hoarding as their centre forward drags a great chance wide.

I realise, with horror, that just one goal could force extra time, and I've arranged to meet my wife back in town. I don't think she'll appreciate hanging around Darlington town centre until six. I daren't entertain the thought of penalties. To my great relief, it turns out that the Darlington fan is proven wrong. It's Town who score the late goal as Kerry wins the ball in midfield and cracks a shot past the keeper. Thomson's in on goal to the right of him, but he was never going to pass it. I like this new ruthless streak.

Trooping out of the ground back into town with the home fans after the match, I hear some admiration for our crisp, sharp passing on the ground. There's also an acknowledgement that Darlington were well beaten. You'll find no argument from me.

I'm pleased Town have approached this tie in the right way, as the victory should keep confidence high heading into the fixture at Ebbsfleet next week. I won't be there though, as I'll be in the Midlands. I don't have any relatives in far flung Kent.

Town up to second as my trip down memory lane is blown off course

Ebbsfleet United (A) W 2-0. Goals: Hall, Muldoon. Crowd: 822.
Article originally published on Thursday 23rd January 2020 under the title *'Harrogate keep up the pressure at the top as I take a trip down memory lane.'*

The excitement levels in this family were off the scale over the weekend as Town's win at Ebbsfleet moved them briefly up to second place, level on points with leaders Barrow. Yes, the Cumbrians have two matches in hand and managed to beat Bromley later in the evening, but Town are the *'form team at the moment'* as announced by Jeff Stelling on Sky Sports.

Whilst Town haven't had the toughest of starts to the New Year, they seem to have learned how to win matches they're expected to win, and that's all they can do to keep the pressure on the leaders. As Simon Weaver succinctly put it on Radio York a couple of weeks ago, Barrow are on an unbeaten run of fifteen matches, but they still can't shake off the teams behind them, so how must they feel? Sooner or later, their luck must change and Town are doing all they can to be there or thereabouts when it does.

I sent last week's column to a Darlington supporting friend, now living in Ilkley. He read the bit about the Town banner being stolen and emailed back to tell me that the same thing had happened to the Boston United flag, or Harrogate Town Reserves' flag if you wish. Although Town fans managed to retrieve our banner, the Boston fans weren't so fortunate, so some of the Darlington fans clubbed together to buy them a new one. It was a nice gesture, and I wished I'd put some money in the collection bucket for ground improvements now.

Finding myself in the West Midlands this weekend, I decided to take a trip down memory lane, making the two mile bus journey back to my hometown to see Gornal Athletic, a team based six levels below Harrogate Town. I haven't seen them play for around thirty five years, even though I keep half an eye on their results.

When I was growing up as a teenager, my grandad lived in a flat overlooking their Garden Walk Stadium. It sounds posh, but it was adjacent to a council estate. I'd spend most weekends and many week nights watching football on their ground. When there wasn't a match, I'd spend hours kicking a ball into one of the goals on the ground, playing out imaginary match-winning scenarios in my head until it got dark, or until hunger set in. Unusually for a team at such a lowly level, they had a huge bank of terracing due to the pitch being several metres below the club house and car park, so there was plenty of room for the fifty or so fans that turned up to watch them in the mid to late seventies.

My grandad had been a miner and a bricklayer and often struggled for breath, using an inhaler into old age. He was fairly housebound and never went to the matches. He'd give me money for football stickers and sweets and often let me have a glass of his homemade wine. Safely out of sight of my parents, it was our little secret. Living on his own, he always looked forward to my frequent visits and I always looked forward to seeing him.

I'd watch many of the matches from an upstairs window in the flat complex he lived in. If I went to the ground, I'd sneak in through one of the many gaps in the rusty, corrugated iron perimeter fence. The old programmes I still own were picked up, having been discarded on the terraces, rusty staples, footmarks and all. One of them still contains the best excuse ever for losing a game badly. And I quote…

'After our recent improved performances we slipped last week when we were blown off course by Gale Force Winds in the last twenty minutes. However, we are not blaming the elements entirely for there was also some poor defensive play which lead to two of the Brereton goals…'

Simon Weaver take note, there's how to write a Manager's column.

At that time, Gornal Athletic were at a level higher in the West Midlands Premier, but every year bought a new relegation battle and victories were scarce in amongst the heavy home defeats on a boggy pitch. Leeson, Farmer and Derrick were heroes to me at the time, and the names stay implanted in my brain. It didn't matter that they were shipping five goals at home to Alvechurch.

Gornal are still in their perpetual relegation battle in the lower Division One this weekend but, when I arrive at the entrance gates in a state of nervous excitement (the gaps in the fence have long since been fixed), there's no one around and the turnstiles are locked. I check my phone to find out that the match has been called off following an early morning pitch inspection. I can't help but feel that it would have been played thirty five years ago.

I decide to take a walk down to my grandad's old flat. He sadly passed away in 1982, but the memories of the times I spent there watching football are precious. I want to create similar happy memories for myself and my daughter, and to never again take the moments we have together watching Town for granted. Wait, did I say *'again'*?

Shortly after Molly started coming to Town every week with me, I remarked to the aforementioned friend of mine in Ilkley, that I was jealous of the fact that his son liked the same music as he did, and of the connection they had through that, whereas my daughter hated all of my music, with the exception of the Undertones' *'Teenage Kicks'*.

My friend's response?

'You go to the football with your daughter. I'm jealous of you.'

Wrexham celebrate the scalp of little old Harrogate Town

Wrexham (H) L 0-2. Crowd: 2,415. Article originally published on Thursday 30th January 2020 under the title *'A first loss in seven, but I'm still left pondering on what might have been.'*

Walking to the ground past rows of parked cars in the Saints, I turn into the narrow, fence-lined ginnel towards Wetherby Road. It's busier than usual and reverberates with chatter. Town, second in the National League, are entertaining Wrexham and it's going to be a good crowd. You can sense it.

Town have won the last six and haven't conceded in over seven and a half hours, but it's our sixth game against Wrexham since we entered the National League and we're yet to win one. Something surely has to give.

It looks like that hoodoo is in for a thrashing today, as a confident and dangerous-looking Town team spray the ball around early doors. Wrexham are reduced to chasing shadows and defending in depth. It's the fastest start we've seen in a while and, to these eyes, it brings back memories of some of the early performances in the promotion season two years ago. Then it all changes briefly.

Wrexham win a free kick in a dangerous position, just outside the far penalty area and, as soon as the ball leaves the Wrexham player's boot, curling around the Town wall as it does, you know it's going into the top corner. It's a great goal, completely against the run of play.

Knocked back, though undeterred, Town resume the siege of the Welsh goal, but a mixture of bad luck, the post, the goalkeeper, last ditch defending, unlucky ricochets, and the complete absence of a clinical edge, conspire to keep the score at 0-1. If we had a twenty goal a season striker, we'd be running away with this league. It's not helped by visiting players falling over like an episode of *Casualty* at every available opportunity and the goalkeeper time-wasting from almost the first minute.

Perversely, Belshaw twice brilliantly keeps us in the game at the end of the first period, as Wrexham threaten again. I was upset that the referee had only added on an additional five minutes, but it now seems like a blessing in disguise. It feels like it might be shaping up to be *'another one of those days'*.

I've spent almost the entire first half watching from the 1919 end, whilst Molly and her friends came in late and stayed in the Kop. *'I've got the Galaxy Caramels,'* I text. It works a treat, as three faces appear in the crowd next to me.

Reunited in the Kop for the second half, we look forward to Town repeating the first half performance, whilst adding goals, but it's Wrexham who come out the strongest and, again, we have man-of-the-match-Belshaw to thank. Town look, well, decidedly worn out and a little disjointed after their first half exertions. The fans call for someone off the bench to change the dynamic. Loan signing Harratt eventually comes on for his home debut but, before he has a chance to get involved, Town find themselves two goals down and you can see heads drop.

From then on, Wrexham are happy to hold on to what they've got, and take advantage of a weak referee by using every trick in the book to frustratingly break play up and run the clock down. To be fair, Town don't look like pulling it back, but it's a professional, if slightly cynical, performance from the visitors. A visiting player will win a foul, the Wrexham players will then surround the referee, arguing for what seems like an age whilst leaving the ball in a remote location, before the furthest player away idles slowly over to retrieve the ball and take it to the correct spot, for the keeper to then take an absolute age to take the free kick. Eventually, the referee books the keeper, but it's too little, too late, as is the entrance of Kiernan, eleven minutes from time.

To see the Wrexham fans wildly celebrating the scalp of little old Harrogate Town is testament to Town's success this season, and should provide me with a little comfort, but it doesn't. That's three home games I've been to against Wrexham and the visitors' net hasn't rippled once.

The one bright side is that no one around us wins, although Barrow gain a point. Again, I could take comfort from this, but all I can think is that if we'd won today, we'd have been one point off top and five clear of third. My glass is decidedly half-empty. Meanwhile, Wrexham join Fylde and Salford in 'The List Of Sides That Harrogate Just Can't Beat No Matter What.' I'm not counting the Trophy match a couple of seasons ago, when Town beat a Wrexham reserve side, brilliant though it was.

Oh well, there's always next week, we're still second in the table and we've not got to face Wrexham again. You see, things are looking up already.

Somewhere in amongst missing flags and an unexpected phone call, a match breaks out

Aldershot Town (A) D 1-1. Goal: Kerry. Crowd: 1,704. Article originally published on Thursday 6th February 2020 under the title *'Shot's chairman's offer to replace stolen Town flags is a great gesture.'*

It all started quite innocently with a tweet from Jack Wilkinson, a Town fan on the coach back from Aldershot. *'Did anyone pick the flags up at today's game? Both have gone missing.'*

The two flags had last been seen when they were taken down from the back of the stand at the Recreation Ground on the final whistle, folded and left next to a steward.

Three hours later, the mystery was solved, as pictures of the missing flags were displayed on the Twitter accounts of two Aldershot fans, one pinned on a dartboard and the other being held up by someone with an emoji disguised face. They'd been stolen whilst the Town fans were clapping the players off, and everyone had assumed that someone else had picked them up.

Polite requests for the flags to be returned were met with sarcasm and abuse, so a number of us, myself and Molly included, set about reporting the incident to the Hampshire club via various channels, asking them what they were going to do about it in the process.

Meanwhile online, things were beginning to get heated, with Boreham Wood and Brackley fans weighing in on Town fans' behalf. One Town fan remarked that hopefully the two Aldershot fans would wake up regretting it in the morning, but a quick perusal of the offending Twitter accounts revealed that self-awareness and remorse may be two commodities in short supply. We weren't dealing with the sharpest tools in the box.

So it was, that I arrived home from work this evening.

'You've got an answer machine message from some football-related person,' my wife says as I enter the house.

'Who?' I ask.

'I don't know, but he left his number and wants you to phone him back.' It turns out to be the Aldershot chairman, Shahid Azeem. I collect the dog and phone him on our regular route. The chairman that is, not the dog. I leave a message.

Half an hour later Shahid returns my call, on his way back from the Houses of Parliament in Central London, whilst I'm stood in a muddy field. He's very apologetic and extremely hacked off with the whole incident. I try to play it all down, after all it's only flags, no one's been hurt and I don't feel he should have to take the flak for a couple of idiots. He tells me that the club will be paying for new flags to be made and I tell him that, although it's a really nice gesture and really appreciated, he shouldn't have to. We end up having a nice chat about football in general and he invites me to call him if I make it to Aldershot next year. I tell him I don't intend to because I'm hoping Town go up.

Later Garry Plant, Town's Managing Director, copies me into an email he's written to the Aldershot chairman, stating *'The measure of any character is not the problem or adversity they face but rather the manner in which they deal with matters ... May we take this opportunity to thank you for your stance and your refreshing approach.'* I couldn't agree more.

So what did those two Aldershot fans achieve exactly? Aside from looking stupid, for glorifying the theft of a banner belonging to a fourteen year-old fan and a supporters' club banner, depicting two hands shaking in friendship, here were two people implicating themselves as suspects online at the same time. They've now wasted the time of people at both Aldershot and Harrogate; time which could have been much better spent, and cost their own club money in the process. I can only think they thought it was a good idea in the spur of the moment. Let's hope contact from the club or CCTV footage from inside the ground may finally give them real cause for remorse.

On the positive side I've learned that, despite the occasional appearance to the contrary, most people are basically good at heart. Witness both Alex Bradley and Ryan Fallowfield offering to pay for a new flag for the fan who'd lost his, and the Aldershot response. Hopefully it's brought the two clubs closer together, and I wish them and their chairman well for the rest of the season.

Yes, decent people outweigh the idiots, loud as they may be. It's just a shame the decent people are left to put right the mess the idiots have created.

And the match? I listened to it online for the first time, tuning into Barry Parker on Radio York for the first half and the local Aldershot commentary for the second; a brilliant development made possible by the fact that the BBC are phasing out their AM channels. And, whilst it sounded like we had the same problems of a lack of ruthlessness in front of goal, a fact rightly acknowledged by Simon Weaver after the match, we remain a tight second. Meanwhile the title remains Barrow's to lose.

It's worth taking a step back here, though, and listening to the thoughts of the BBC Surrey commentators. Describing it as the best match of the season at the Recreation Ground, they didn't want it to end, were very complimentary about the way Town played, and were extremely pleased with the point and the way the home team battled to hang on for it at the end. Sometimes we can get too embroiled in the negatives and it takes others to point out the positives.

Footnote: 9:55pm Tuesday evening. Dover 2 Barrow 1. An 88th minute winner from our very own Michael Woods inflicts the first defeat for Barrow since October in the league. Hope springs eternal. Let's hope our rivals enjoy the long trip back up to Cumbria.

Victory on two fronts: whisper it, Town look the real deal

Eastleigh (H) (FA Trophy Third Round) W 2-0. Goals: Bradley, Emmett. Crowd: 947. Yeovil Town (H) W 3-0. Goals: Thomson 2, Diamond. Crowd: 801. Article originally published on Thursday 13th February 2020 under the title *'A team of Town's quality deserves to be playing in front of bigger crowds.'*

Entering the ground at the 1919 end these days feels like a bit of a novelty. There's no enforced segregation inside the ground and so we take up our positions in the tea bar end of the Wetherby Road stand for the Eastleigh FA Trophy match, just like the old days. *'It's a much better view here,'* agree Molly and her friends. One very vocal visiting fan, in a blue and white bobble hat, plants himself at the front of the home choir to enjoy the game, even though his team are attacking the far end, and a nice bit of banter ensues.

I've no time for teams putting out a second string eleven in a cup match. If Liverpool aren't going to take the FA Cup seriously, for example, kick them out I say. Controversial, I know, but there you go. I think we've firmly established though that Town making six changes doesn't mean they're fielding a weaker team, not when the players coming in can count themselves unlucky to be out of the starting eleven in the first place. Moving Burrell and Bradley into their favoured midfield positions to make room for Fallowfield and George

Outside Wetherspoons, Yeovil, October 2019. *(Jack Wilkinson)*

Singing in the seats at Yeovil, something Simon Weaver later recalled as giving the team a huge lift that day. *(Matt Kirkham)*

Mutual applause at Yeovil.

At Halifax again, this time in the FA Cup, October 2019. *(Matt Kirkham)*

Jack Emmett fires in the late winning goal against Aldershot Town, October 2019... *(Matt Kirkham)*

...and wheels away towards the Kop to celebrate. *(Matt Kirkham)*

The visit of Portsmouth in the FA Cup First Round, November 2019. *(Matt Kirkham)*

Ryan Fallowfield scores a wonder goal against Chesterfield in the mist, November 2019. *(Matt Kirkham)*

In front of the murals at Victory Park, Chorley, December 2019.

Victory Park, Chorley, December 2019.

On the way to the Raglan Quoit, Hartlepool, January 2020.

Another victory on the road, Hartlepool, January 2020.

Players and management leaving the pitch after the FA Trophy
victory at Darlington, January 2020, and a rare instance of
Matt Kirkham appearing in somebody else's photo.

A view from the away end at AFC Fylde during Storm Jorge in the
FA Trophy, February 2020. Note the Fylde fans (what's left of them)
huddled into the back of the stand to escape the elements.

Jack Muldoon wheels away after putting Town in front in the FA Trophy Quarter Final at AFC Fylde, February 2020. *(Matt Kirkham)*

The celebrations in the away end. *(Matt Kirkham)*

James Belshaw celebrating with the travelling fans after Town's thrilling 4-3 win at Chesterfield, March 2020. *(Matt Kirkham)*

George Thomson scores Town's first ever goal at Wembley Stadium, as Notts County are defeated 3-1 in the National League Play-Off Final, August 2020. *(Matt Kirkham)*

Town players and staff celebrate winning the National League Play-Off Final in front of an empty Wembley Stadium. *(Matt Kirkham)*

Scenes of celebration at the open top bus parade, York Place, Harrogate, August 2020. *(Steve Riding)*

Smith in the full back positions isn't a weakening of the team in my opinion. It's also a good chance to look at the two new squad additions.

The seventeen year old centre forward, Kian Harratt, exhibits no little confidence for his tender years and displays a willingness to strike at goal from anywhere; witness a bullet-like snap shot rattling the post in the first half. He looks to be the sort of player that thrives off making runs off the back of the last defender and it just needs Town players to spot him in these positions more. It's a promising full debut indeed, capped by an assist for Bradley's opening goal, a first time shot whistling past the stranded keeper. If I have one criticism of Town, it's that the players often take one touch too many in front of goal, so these developments are encouraging.

Defensively, Maxim Kouogun slots in seamlessly alongside the dependable Will Smith, and becomes an instant crowd favourite. He's not easily shaken off, snuffing out danger, whilst keeping his eye fixed firmly on the ball. It's hard to believe he hasn't played a competitive match since November, although he'll undoubtedly have bigger tests. The Town faithful cobble a song together off the back of a fag packet and he's serenaded with it at the end when he comes over to applaud the Kop.

The visitors are finally put to bed when Emmett comes on and threads home four minutes from time. *'We're the famous Harrogate Town and we're off to Wem-ber-lee,'* we sing, followed by *'It's a long way back to Eastleigh when you've lost.'* The bobble hat-headed Eastleigh fan, who's come round with us to the Kop for the second half, decides to make his way back round the ground to his own fans. He applauds the Kop, and we applaud him back. After the stolen banners distraction of last week, this is football back to how it should be.

It's an all-round comprehensive performance, leaving Simon Weaver with a selection headache ahead of the big promotion six-pointer on Tuesday night.

One thing in table-topping Barrow's favour up till now has been the unwelcoming, inhospitable nature of their ground, based as it is out in the middle of nowhere, a chilling gale blowing in off the Irish Sea, heavy pitch and a team from deepest Essex really not fancying it. In contrast, Harrogate offers a fat rascal and cucumber sandwiches, with the crust cut off at Betty's.

Well, not tonight. One day after Storm Ciara. I get back in from taking the dog out, having endured driving sheets of horizontal frozen rain, lashing against my face, and even I'm not fancying the ten minute walk to the ground. It must be cold, as Molly's friend, Lily, has the scarf I gave her on for the first time this season.

As it turns out, the manager leaves the two goal scorers, Bradley and Emmett, out of the team to face Yeovil, in favour of Fallowfield and Thomson. It's a tough call, but one that's justified on the night, as these two cause havoc down the Yeovil right, working together to get in behind the defence on a number of occasions.

Yeovil are a shadow of the team we encountered down in Somerset and, after a quiet opening twenty minutes, Town take charge. The same problem of not taking chances leads me to start worrying that it might be one of those nights, but almost on the stroke of half-time, Thomson controls and prods in after great work by Muldoon on the left wing.

I'm half expecting an onslaught from the visitors, now playing with the wind in the second half, but it never materialises. Town score early through Diamond and control the second half. Once the third goes in, Yeovil start disintegrating in front of our very eyes. There's still time for the dismissal of a visiting player for a horrible challenge on Will Smith and a comedy of errors across the Yeovil back four on a number of occasions, played out to a background of sarcastic cheers from the Town fans.

The fact the visiting manager unjustly called Town *'negative'* in a severe case of sour grapes, after our 2-1 win at their place, isn't lost on the Kop, who spend much of the latter part of the second half reminding him of this in no uncertain terms. He goes on to describe his team's performance as *'woeful'* and *'toothless'* in an interview where he looks like he's lost a tenner and found a penny, although he can still hardly bear to give Harrogate any praise at all.

Whisper it, Town look the real deal tonight. It's just a shame more people aren't here to witness it.

The only dampener on one of the best performances of the season is the attendance. Whilst there's a fair contingent of a hundred or so brave souls up from Yeovil, the home turnout appears lower than the weekend. It's a hugely disappointing crowd for such a crunch match. The release of average attendance figures this week shows the Town average over 200 down on last season, placing us 19th in the attendance league, with all the big away followings having already been and gone. The crowd tonight turns out to be fully 532 below this season's average. I know we've had a rapid rise from 250 hardy souls at home, but this team really does deserve to be playing in front of higher numbers.

Not happy when it rains. Fruitless journeys and the *'Worton curse'*

Barnet (A) (abandoned at half-time). Article originally published on Thursday 20th February 2020 under the title *'Travelling fans' visit to North London turns into the dampest of damp squibs.'*

There's an ancient saying in our house that goes something like *'Now you've put the Worton curse on it.'* This *'Worton curse'* started many years ago, when I developed the habit of inadvertently predicting somewhere would be closed, or something would be sold out, long before we got to visit such place, or purchase said item, thus rendering the entire journey a waste of time. It got so bad that my wife forbade me from uttering phrases such as *'I bet it'll be out of stock,'* before we set off, for fear of inviting the worst.

So I instinctively knew the Barnet match on Tuesday night was doomed, the moment commentator Barry Parker uttered the immortal words *'If the rain continues like this it will not finish,'* barely six minutes into the first half. It appears that Barry also has the gift of the curse.

With Town still in the FA Trophy, the potential is there for a minor fixture pile-up towards the end of the season, so I initially welcomed the decision to reschedule the match so quickly after Saturday's postponement. That is, until I saw the saturated state of the Barnet pitch in a supporter's post on the following Sunday.

Now, with the benefit of hindsight, it was always a risky decision and, ultimately the wrong one, as the match was halted at half-time with the score at 1-1. So spare a thought for the Town supporters who took the afternoon off work to travel down to North London.

With the coach from Saturday cancelled, fourteen fans squeezed into a minibus kindly loaned by the club. They set off in good time at 3pm, only to arrive at the ground five minutes late due to a closure of the A1. On arrival, they had to queue for five minutes in the pouring rain at the ticket office to get in. As I write this, they're due back in Harrogate at 1.30am, having witnessed barely 35 minutes of football, missing George Thomson's first minute 'goal' in the process.

I couldn't travel on the Saturday, but I'm on holiday from work this week. Not being in the know, I'd assumed there was no organised transport down to Barnet and so continued with business as usual, safe in the knowledge there was no way I could get there and back in one day.

Business as usual consisted of my wife and I going to Guiseley to pick up some picture frames, to Kirkstall to buy chips from our favourite chippy, to Headingley to visit an antique centre and to Tesco (oh joy) in Seacroft, to pick up some school shirts for Molly. I often see it as a badge of honour that Harrogate is the only postcode in the country without a Tesco superstore, but not in times like these.

To cut a long story short, the picture frames had been discontinued, the chip shop was shuttered up and the antique centre didn't open on Tuesdays. Unfortunately, Tesco was open, shirts in stock, thus rendering the day only slightly less pointless. For once though, I'd not foreseen any of this coming. I must be losing my powers.

Fortunately, my wasted day involved me travelling no further than the north side of Leeds. Thank goodness I hadn't gotten wind of the minibus and tried to get a place on it. I feel I dodged a bullet in that respect.

Continuing on the subject of fruitless journeys, the masochist in me switched over to BBC Radio Cumbria at half-time, hoping that lightning would strike twice and Dover would do us another favour at Barrow. It didn't and neither did they.

It turns out, though, that the commentating team had a sweepstake on the number of visiting fans. The winner predicted thirteen. There were ten. Can there be a longer journey to watch a football match on a Tuesday night than that this season?

Staying firmly on the issue of travel, this week has seen the rescheduling of our match at Solihull Moors from Saturday afternoon to the preceding Friday night. The home team are trying to *'maximise the potential for bigger crowds'*, their words not mine, and the original date clashed with West Brom v Birmingham and Aston Villa v Chelsea. I can understand Solihull's motives, but the surprise for me is that Town agreed to the move, especially bearing in mind the problems supporters will have getting down there in the Friday afternoon rush hour. That's if they can get the time off work again.

'£20 says the attendance will be no different to had it been played on the Saturday,' commented one fan in the discussion online, showing a healthy display of cynicism long since banned in our house. I'm tempted to agree, others may not, but his money's safe, as this is a bet that will be pretty hard to prove either way.

Life's a gamble. My hard-earned money's on Ryan Fallowfield

Eastleigh (H) W 3-0. Goals: Falkingham, Diamond, Muldoon. Crowd: 1,249. Article originally published on Thursday 27th February 2020 under the title *'Sacrifice required in order to secure my daughter sought-after Town shirt.'*

'How much are you planning to spend?' my wife asks before the Eastleigh game.

'I reckon around 25 to £30,' I reply, not having the slightest clue really.

'Well ok, but don't go over the top,' comes the response.

You see, there's a charity auction of shirts worn by the Town players last season, and it's taking place directly after the match.

Very happy with another comprehensive home win and another clean sheet, putting the pressure on Barrow kicking off at 5:20, we head for the clubhouse behind the goal. As we wait for the auction to begin, my daughter and her friend are pretty excited on witnessing most of the players enter the bar after the match. I don't know why, it's not as if they don't see them often.

Molly's after either Jack Emmett's or Ryan Fallowfield's shirt. Trouble is, these may be two of the more expensive ones, as both players are still at the club and fairly popular to boot. We sit down, wait, and discuss tactics.

'*Why don't you bid?*' I say to Molly, figuring rival bidders might let her win one more easily than me.

'*No, you do it for me,*' she replies.

To be honest, I've never been to any kind of auction before and I'm a little bit apprehensive with all this responsibility resting on my shoulders.

It's the away shirts up for auction first. Behind the auctioneer, Barrow are on the big screen, playing at Sutton. A cheer goes up, and the auctioneer looks a little surprised, it turns out that Barrow have had a 'goal' disallowed.

We've already decided we're going for the home shirts, so I'm a little bit worried when some of the blue away ones start to go for serious money.

Cue pantomime boos when Callum Howe's old shirt comes up for auction.

'*£15... will anyone offer me £20?*' pleads the auctioneer through his dodgy microphone. There's no interest.

'*Sold for £15. I've got another one of these,*' he points out, to another chorus of pantomime boos.

Bizarrely, the second one goes on to sell for more.

Cue real boos, as Barrow go first one and then two up on the big screen.

Josh Falkingham's away shirt is offered for sale. '*Have you got any of those in extra-large?*' shouts one wag from the floor. It disappears for a bargain £25. I later learn that it's too small for the buyer's ten year old son, so it's now being proudly worn by his seven year old daughter. You just couldn't make this stuff up.

Meanwhile, I manage to persuade Molly that it may be best to bid on someone else's shirt, as we may get it cheaper.

'What about Joe Leesley's away shirt?' I suggest. *'We're not bidding above £20,'* she says. It sells for five pounds more.

She quite fancies Dom Knowles' old home shirt, so we decide to try for that later. His away shirt comes up first. There's a £50 bid in from an anonymous internet bidder, probably Dom Knowles himself for all I know. Best laid plans and all that.

'What about Aaron Williams' shirt? I reason, *'It could have been the shirt he was wearing when he scored at Southport to send us to the top of the National League.'*

'No,' comes the reply.

Eventually we get round to the home shirts. If there's one thing in our favour, it's that the crowd in the bar has thinned and the auctioneer seems to be speeding up.

There are more pantomime boos for Howe, whilst Langmead's shirt goes for a knockdown price. Unfortunately, there's another anonymous £50 internet bid in for Dom Knowles' home shirt. Someone must have a crush on him.

'Shall I bid £52?' I ask.

'No, it's too much,' Molly responds firmly.

Falkingham goes for good money, and then it's Emmett. I'm ready.

'Don't appear too keen,' I tell Molly. A minute later I'm bidding £50. Then, after a pause, when I think I have it, someone outbids me.

'Can I ask you for £57?' asks the auctioneer in scenes reminiscent of the Monty Python *'Mr Creosote'* sketch, where the waiter, John Cleese, tempts the bloated diner with a

'wafer thin mint', before diving over the pot plants in the restaurant to avoid the subsequent explosion.

I look at Molly, tempted. *'Shall we?'*

'No, it's too much,' she replies yet again. The banker has spoken.

Sutton pull a goal back, to cheers in the bar.

Burrell's home shirt sells for £45, and the winning bidder promptly gives it to one of the young Town fans in front of him, who's been trying unsuccessfully to win a shirt all night for £10 and had wanted this one so much, that he'd gone up to £40 to secure it.

Then it's Fallowfield's turn. I think Molly's given up getting a shirt at this stage. It's our last chance and, before I know it, I'm bidding £50 again, expecting the bloke I'm bidding against to go higher, but he doesn't. After what seems like an eternity, it's ours. The look on Molly's face is worth every penny, even though I've broken our budget to get it.

It's a bargain, compared to what happens later, when Thomson's home shirt nearly hits three figures in a bidding frenzy. Now I've just got to justify that amount to my wife.

Molly goes back to break the 'good' news whilst I head to the Co-op to get some money out of the cash point. I wouldn't mind, but when I eventually return to hand over the dosh for the shirt, part of the stitching is loose on the back of the neck. If it wasn't for charity, I'd be asking for a discount. I can only hope the thing's been laundered.

'Tell me Molly's having me on...' says my wife as I enter through the front door, *'... £50 on a shirt?'*

I go for the heart-strings option, *'You should have seen the look on your daughter's face when we won it. I couldn't let her leave without a shirt, it was a really difficult situation.'* It seems to work.

'Barrow only drew two each!' shouts Molly excitedly down the stairs.

Even so, I decide to put a treasured rare seven inch single* on the internet later that night to compensate and, barely one hour later, it's disappeared from my life forever for twice the amount of Fallowfield's shirt.

The sacrifices you make for your kids.

Footnote: The auction raised over a thousand pounds for Harrogate Town AFC Community Foundation and 120 Marathon Man. Thanks to Jordan Ford for his input into this column.

*Anti-Cimex's 'Victims Of A Bomb Raid' EP on Malign Massacre Records. I'd owned it since the seminal Swedish hardcore punk band played Leeds in 1984. When I told Molly this, she said she felt really bad. So she should. Although I'm not telling her I have a discography LP with all the tracks duplicated on it anyway, and I'd appreciate it if you didn't either.

Town take on Storm Jorge and slay the Fylde curse

AFC Fylde (A) (FA Trophy Quarter Final) W 3-2. Goals: Kerry, Muldoon 2. Crowd: 1,281. Article originally published on Thursday 5th March 2020 under the title *'Town defy Storm Jorge to finally break the Fylde curse - and in some style, too.'*

If you'd asked me to pick a tie I didn't want for the quarter final of the FA Trophy, it would most certainly have been Fylde away. Town haven't beaten them in eleven previous attempts, a run going back to a time before my daughter and I started supporting the club. They've knocked us out of the play-offs twice and, even when on the ropes earlier in the season, they conspired to snatch a point from the jaws of defeat, thanks to a jobsworth of a linesman spotting the flimsiest of hand balls.

Nonetheless, if we're going to get to Wembley, today's the day we have to lay that Fylde curse to rest.

We set off from Wetherby Road on the, shall we say, more sedate of the two supporters' coaches. You know it's going to be a quiet journey when you get on and find that the back seats aren't taken. Not that we took them either, all that bouncing around at the back makes me feel sick.

It's not the weather for a football match on the beach, as witnessed before the league encounter in August, especially with Storm Jorge on the way. So this time, Town fans have received an invite to the Fylde local, the Stanley Arms, a homely pub in the shade of the Fox's biscuit factory in nearby Wesham.

Two pints, two halves of lemonade, a basket of chips and three Leeds goals on the telly later, we set off to the ground, having graduated to the noisier coach of the two for the short journey.

Although the sun's shining when we arrive, there's a vicious wind blowing towards the far goal. Town kick off in that direction, but fail to puncture the defence of a home team struggling to get out of their own half against the conditions. Spoilt by the weather, the underwhelming nature of the first half gives no hint of the drama to come.

When Town go one down against the wind within eight minutes of the restart, I suffer that familiar sinking feeling that goes with watching us play Fylde. But this Town team is currently made of sterner stuff.

Somehow, don't ask me how, Town manage to battle their way up the pitch and start to have a real go at Fylde. We roar them on from the shelter of the away end and, cometh the hour, cometh the man. Ex-Fylde player Muldoon enters the fray and, within five minutes, dances his way past two defenders in the area to set up an in-rushing Kerry for the equaliser. Barely a minute later, Kerry drives into the heart of the home defence and returns the favour.

The Town end goes crazy, and even a yellow card for jumping into the crowd can't wipe the smile off Muldoon's face.

Not for nothing, though, do we refer to the Fylde curse. Just as we think we might come away with a famous win, Storm Jorge, in all its force, rolls into town. Horizontal sheets of wind and rain flatten the corner flags and batter Town back into their own area. I've never seen anything like it at a football match before.

The Town goal proceeds to lead a charmed life as Fylde and Storm Jorge attack. Yet following a rousing seven minute rendition of 'Town All Over' from the travelling supporters, it looks like we might have literally weathered the storm. Molly moves down to the front, with one minute to go, to clap the jubilant players on the final whistle. Me, I know better and stay firmly put, biting my nails.

'I can't believe we're going to finally beat the Fylde curse,' says my daughter to the fan next to her. The words have barely left her mouth, when their full back despairingly decides to have a pot shot from thirty yards. It catches the storm and flies past Cracknell like a bullet. Extra time it is then.

The teams turn round again and, for the first time in the match, Town make the elements count, albeit in the most bizarre of fashions. The Fylde keeper kicks the ball out of his hands, it reaches high above the half way line before the wind boomerangs it back in mid-air towards Muldoon, facing away from goal, thirty yards out. Without a second thought, he turns and hits a dipping volley over the bemused keeper.

This time, Town hold out against Storm Jorge by the skin of their teeth, with free kicks from the half way line landing on the top of the net and our hosts lashing over from four yards. Thank goodness there's no Danny Rowe in the home team to take advantage.

Cue wild celebrations in the away end at the final whistle. The curse has finally been vanquished. The players head over joyously but briefly, before heading for the sanctuary of the tunnel to thaw out, and who can blame them? Molly and I, fully wrapped up against the wind and rain, can barely face to walk five minutes home on disembarking from the coach, let alone run around in flimsy shirt and shorts kicking a football for over two hours.

*Tuesday 22nd September 2020. Town have just beaten Notts County 1-0 in front of an empty Meadow Lane in the semi-final of the FA Trophy; six and a half long months after this quarter-final match was played. Molly and I watched it on YouTube. The contrast in atmosphere and excitement, when compared with the AFC Fylde quarter-final victory, couldn't have been starker. It makes me miss going to football desperately. A date with Concord Rangers awaits us in the Wembley Final. When this will be played is, as yet, unclear, as the intention is not to stage it until supporters are allowed back into stadia, and plans to allow this from the 1st October have just been put on hold for the foreseeable future.

Fun, fun, fun in Chesterfield whilst waiting for the clampdown

Chesterfield (A) W 4-3. Goals: Stead 2, Thomson, Muldoon. Crowd: 2,912. Bromley (H) D 1-1. Goal: Diamond. Crowd: 1,339. Article originally published on Thursday 12th March 2020 under the title *'The future is uncertain in more ways than one due to spread of coronavirus.'*

With the depressing news this week of the slow spread of Covid-19 worldwide and the subsequent nationwide lockdown in Italy, we currently find ourselves looking into an uncertain future. How things are going to pan out is anyone's guess, but it seems fairly certain that things are going to get a whole lot worse before getting better. Only time will tell what sort of restrictions we see placed on domestic football, and whether we see people choosing to self-isolate in such circumstances.

To this end, we have to take our enjoyment where and when we can, so I'll start this column with a joyous re-telling of the Chesterfield victory a week ago.

It's Tuesday evening, and we're heading down to Derbyshire on a full coach. It's going to be a late night for Molly, but I won't tell school if you don't. On arrival, a full hour early, there's not a lot to do other than visit the sprawling retail park next door. There's a huge Tesco, accessed via one of those flat escalators for trolleys, so we amuse ourselves by walking backwards on it, only to find ourselves being stared at in bemusement by the locals.

'Haven't they seen anyone having fun before?' I say to Molly when, in reality, the good people of Chesterfield are probably all wondering why people from Harrogate haven't yet learned how to use escalators properly. Suitably fed, watered and amused, we head for Chesterfield's smart new stadium.

The match itself is a pulsating encounter which ebbs and flows in favour of first one team and then the other. When Chesterfield peg Town back to 3-3 with eight minutes to go, it's a huge disappointment, but I manage to settle for a decent point against a dangerous home side. Not so Town.

Chesterfield may have Denton, their towering striker, who is involved in all three goals tonight and virtually unplayable in the air, but Town have Stead and Diamond.

Stead puts away two majestic headers in probably his best game for Town, and Diamond is a revelation.

Having already played a huge part in the first goal, directly assisted the second and third goals, and seen a perfectly good goal chalked off by an unfathomable refereeing decision, you could forgive him for easing off.

But confidence is an infectious thing and, having nearly scored in injury time himself, he once again runs at the weary home defence, before picking out Muldoon in the 93rd minute for the winning goal. There's disbelief and wild abandon in the away end. Last year's one-nil victory here was superb enough, but this blows it out of the ball park.

Such an unbelievable rollercoaster of a victory it is, that it renders me speechless. No easy task, I can tell you. With print deadline looming on the Wednesday morning, I hit writer's block. How on earth can I do justice to what I've just seen, in a rushed hour on the coach journey back? We'd also promised my wife that Molly would get some sleep on the way home. There's absolutely no chance of that.

Moving on to Saturday, things start to get serious. With Barrow losing at home for the first time since September, an evening BT Sports victory for Town, against an out-of-sorts Bromley, will take them to within two points of the summit.

It's obvious Bromley saw the match in mid-week, as every time Diamond receives the ball he's immediately surrounded by two or three visiting players. I find myself screaming out for Town to stretch the Bromley defence by using Thomson, often in space, on the opposite right wing.

After a tight, goalless first half, it looks like my prayers have been answered early in the second. Muldoon finally gets in down the right and crosses for Diamond to sweep the ball into the net in front of a noisy Kop. The sense of sheer excitement, coupled with relief, is palpable. It looks like Town might blow the visitors away with their intensity for an all-too-brief spell, but gradually Bromley take control, as Town struggle to get out of their own half with any meaningful possession.

It still looks like we may hang on for a famous victory, but a late equalising own goal punctures our dreams. All of a sudden, there's hardly a sound in the Kop. Never have I heard it go so deathly quiet, so quickly.

Disappointing though it is, it's no more than the visitors deserve, and I can't help feeling that the exertions at Chesterfield in midweek have taken their toll on the Town players. Bromley may be on a bad run, but they're still a decent team, and that's twice this season they've pegged us back from winning positions.

So the week ends in a tale of two late goals, one cancelling the other out.

It's undoubtedly a lost opportunity to put more pressure on Barrow. But, in fairness, the league is never going to be decided over one weekend in early March. There's still a long way to go between now and the end of the season, and there'll be a few twists and turns along the way. The positive aspect is that we've gained another point on the leaders and they've still to come to Wetherby Road. Whoever holds their nerve the best will win it.

Yes, the future is uncertain in more ways than one.

Chapter Four
Tell me when my light turns green

National Lockdown

The fun is over

Article originally published on Thursday 19th March 2020 under the title *'It is too early to say where suspension of the season leaves our beloved Town.'*

Writing this column last week was a difficult balancing act. Football was still playing on, but I could see the coronavirus outbreak approaching fast down the tracks, and my overwhelming feeling was that the football season, indeed normal life itself, was living on borrowed time. Last week's column now seems hopelessly out of date, such has been the pace of change over the last seven days. What I didn't predict was just how quickly things would change in the world of football.

With a government seemingly caught in the headlights with regards to the scale of the problem and the need to act fast, we saw the ludicrous situation of 3,000 Athletico Madrid fans being allowed to travel to Anfield, and drink in the bars, despite the Spanish capital being in effective lockdown and football there being played behind closed doors. Thankfully the FA, Premier League and EFL took the sensible decision to cancel all matches soon after, the day after the government had effectively said *'carry on as normal.'*

We were then left with the unedifying spectacle of the National League dragging its heels and allowing matches to continue last weekend. Quite how they felt it was acceptable to say that Notts County could host Eastleigh and Harrogate

Town's first team travel to Solihull, when even the Harrogate Ladies' fixtures were cancelled, is anyone's guess.

As it turned out, Harrogate sensibly pulled out of the Solihull match on the Friday night, announcing that four members of staff, two players amongst them, were having to self-isolate after feeling unwell. Many of the planned National League fixtures the following day followed suit, although around half were unnecessarily played, until it became blindingly obvious, even to the National League authorities, that the situation was untenable. I'd already made the decision that, should the FA Trophy match against Notts County actually go ahead, I wasn't going to attend anyway. We have to break the lines of transmission of this virus.

So even though we currently find ourselves in the situation where first team fixtures have been suspended until April 4th, I think we can almost certainly predict that the football season is finished past that.

The questions about what happens next, and where we go from here, are not questions that can be answered with any clarity yet.

So where does this leave Harrogate Town? The short answer is that no one knows. Although what we can say with some certainty is that it's undoubtedly been a tremendous season for the club, cruelly cut short just as we were eyeing the possibility of promotion and at least one historic trip to Wembley.

Whilst heading to the shops yesterday, I bumped into my old boss on Oatlands Junction and stated that, having lived and breathed Harrogate Town with my daughter through this column all season, as if it was the most important thing in the

[249]

world, it all now seemed trivial in comparison. I said it but, in hindsight, I don't wholly believe it to be the case.

Although football does indeed pale into insignificance in times like these, it's precisely things like the adventures we've all been through this season that keep us going in normal times, and I'm going to miss watching Town in the near future. We all need to keep these memories close in the weeks ahead, safe in the knowledge that once we do get through this challenging period, normality will return.

To that effect, the news coming out of Town this week, of the signing of Guiseley's Aaron Martin, is heartening, and shows more signs of the club seeking to retain the bulk of its current squad, whilst strengthening where it needs to.

In the meantime, stay safe and look after your loved ones.

Clampdown

Article originally published on Thursday 26th March 2020 under the title *'We've all got to remain disciplined and do our bit to help see off coronavirus.'*

It's only been a week since I last sat down to pen this column but, in terms of developments out in the country, it feels like an eternity. We now find ourselves into the second day of lockdown and, with Covid-19 on the advance, the message couldn't be more stark. Stay at home to save lives.

Following the prime minister's statement, the only reasons to be leaving home are:

· to shop for basic necessities, as infrequently as possible;

· for one form of exercise a day, alone or with members of your household only;

· for medical need, or to provide care or to help a vulnerable person; and

· to travel to and from work, but only where it is absolutely necessary and cannot be done from home.

Yet, as I sit and write on day one of the lockdown, I can still see builders out working on local people's homes, work that just isn't essential at this point in time. Granted, this may change as the lockdown kicks in properly and the government further clarifies its advice as to what work is essential, but it's up to us all to take the initiative and stay at home now. I'm lucky in that I've been working from home for two weeks anyway, and my employer has shut down offices and construction projects for the time being. I know this is easier said than done, but it really is a matter of life and death.

It doesn't help that HS2 and Hinckley Point construction projects were announced as continuing even into lockdown. The government needs to act to close these projects down, so as to set the example for everyone else. Employers may say that best working practices can be adopted on site to put in place social distancing but, working on a construction site, I know this to be almost impossible. You then have to consider the footprint of each worker. Travelling to site invariably involves close contact in vans or on public transport, there may be materials to pick up and petrol stations to visit. In the case of the 1,500 workers at Hinckley Point, many live in temporary shared accommodation close to the site, are bought in together in shifts of 600 on buses and then return to their families, in different parts of the country, at the weekend. This project, and all others like it, should be shut down now.

With regards to leaving home for basic necessities, we all have our part to play here. The less we can shop, the better. This is the most dangerous time, as infection rates spiral rapidly, due to the spread of the virus amongst people pre-lockdown. Everything may seem normal out there, but you don't need to be showing symptoms of the virus to spread it.

To this end, here are a few practical tips we've been employing in this household, especially bearing in mind that supermarkets have been overcrowded and are now only just starting to bring in place social distancing restrictions. Look in your cupboards and freezers and start eating the things you've had kicking around for ages. Don't waste food. Seek out a local company, in need of the business, offering a delivery service. If you do need to go out to buy food, send one person only. Stick to the small local, less-crowded shop if possible, they will appreciate your custom. Before going out, check if you can pick up essentials for someone else in the same trip, for example a vulnerable neighbour. This is just the tip of the iceberg. The key message is, the more you can avoid going out at this point in time, the better.

Now before I start sounding too pious and holier-than-thou, let me tell you a little story regarding my family's weekend.

Last Saturday, before the lockdown kicked in, we decided to take advantage of the kind offer from Fountains Abbey to open free of charge to enable people to get some fresh air. We, like many others, felt it was probably one of the last chances for a while to get out and about, the weather was nice and hell, it was free. We were fully intending to drive there as a family unit, stay at a safe social distance and walk the dog. When we got there the car park was rammed; it was busier than I've ever seen it before. We promptly turned round and left, finding a small empty wood in Nidderdale to walk the dog instead. The next day, Fountains Abbey made the sensible decision to close its gates.

I'd had thoughts of driving out to Almscliffe Crag on the Sunday, reasoning I could social distance and also because I love it. After the Fountains Abbey experience, I made the decision to leave the car on the drive for the foreseeable future and stay local to walk the dog. We've all got to be disciplined and start to set the example going forward if we're to beat this virus, and Fountains Abbey was my real road to Damascus moment.

Whilst multi-tasking isn't my strong point, Molly and I set off for the Stray on Monday evening to walk the dog, armed with a football for exercise, veering into the road to social distance from the occasional person on the way. It's weird, avoiding someone, yet smiling at them at the same time, but it's just something we're going to have to get used to.

We set up goal posts on the Stray whilst the dog kept her distance. After a while, Molly stopped playing and pointed.

'Dad, is that Jack Emmett over there?' she exclaimed in a loud whisper.

I looked over to where she was pointing, and there indeed was Jack, running up and down the Stray, training in isolation. As he ran within a few metres of our goal, I wished him encouragement from a social distance, but he continued straight past, headphones in ears. In hindsight, he was probably avoiding the weirdos staring at him. Under normal circumstances, it would have been great for him to have taken a shot at Molly in goal but, then again, under normal circumstances he'd have been training with the squad at Wetherby Road. However, I can reveal to Simon Weaver that Jack is taking his home-working seriously.

It's the end of the world as we know it, and I'm not sure I feel fine

Article originally published on Thursday 2nd April 2020 under an unknown title; as I forgot to buy* a copy of the *Advertiser* at the time, the newspaper office archives are currently inaccessible as people are still working from home, and somebody's nicked the back copy of that week's edition from the local library.

I was talking to a work colleague on Skype this week. He's always fiercely resisted working from home, but now finds himself easing into a '*bizarre kind of normality.*'

In truth, I'd emailed him for work related reasons and he'd let slip that he was currently working in the kitchen whilst wearing a woollen hat and listening to Part One of the Radio 4 broadcast of '*Stalingrad*' by Vasily Grossman. He's of the older generation, like myself, who'll put three jumpers and a coat on before spending money on the heating. I'd Skyped him to see the hat, and his kitchen. Isn't that what we're all doing currently, looking at each other's interior decor?

'*Tell you what,*' he said '*them Russkies got through plenty of vodka. Even when there was a war on.*'

This reminded me of our outing to the shops for essentials this weekend. Whilst sitting in the car, having been to Pets At Home for supplies and waiting for my wife to emerge from Aldi, where the number of any one item you can buy has been restricted to four, I witnessed a man leaving whilst cradling four bottles of vodka in his arms.

I guess everyone has a different idea of 'essentials'. Mine, when the bread, milk and cheese are unpacked, is creme eggs.

So here we are into the second week of lockdown and I'll be the first to admit that it's been a mix of emotions.

We started in good shape. Molly made pizza and homemade chips and we cooked broccoli and rhubarb from the allotment. We've had time to properly prepare our own meals every day and even make our own bread. I set off intending to read loads of books I've not had time to open, but found myself taking all of one afternoon to properly clean the spare bedroom and most of another day to clean the house windows. I'd cancelled the window cleaner around five years ago to save money, and my wife was constantly threatening to re-employ him, as our new window cleaner always seemed to be at Town matches.

I booked my final two annual leave days from work, and it all seemed a bit pointless, as there was nowhere to go, even if I was allowed to. I even found myself asking my boss for extra work. Normally I'm trying to get rid of it, there's so much.

Then, of course, there's the news. I've always avidly followed, and had an opinion on, current events. Now we're all trying to avoid it in this household, just making sure we update on events once a day, as you can find the gravity of the whole thing quickly starting to overwhelm you.

Once all of this is over and we reach some form of normality, let's not forget the brave, vital role of the health service workers, cleaners, delivery drivers, school staff, supermarket workers, emergency services, postal workers and all the other key workers. Heroes all, who've been hammered in terms of pay and conditions in recent times, but without whom, this country wouldn't run.

The rumours doing the rounds last week regarding the National League season ending now and the current top two, Town and Barrow, being promoted to the Football League were exciting but ultimately not true. Instead it was announced that all leagues below the National League North and South were to be declared null and void and expunged from the records.

Although it's especially hard on teams like South Shields FC, who were 13 points clear and on the way to promotion to National League North, spare a thought for Jersey Bulls who, in their debut season in Division One of the Combined Counties League, had won all 27 matches played and already achieved promotion. Or so they thought.

The National League simply restated its desire to complete the current season *'as quickly as possible'*, trying to present this as some kind of certainty when it clearly wasn't, then suspended it indefinitely. We're in this lockdown for what looks like the long haul. Just ask yourself this... At what point does it become safe enough to allow large gatherings at sports events again? No one has the answer to that question yet.

*No, I don't even get a complimentary copy.

A moment of touching poignancy

Article originally published on Thursday 9th April 2020 under the title *'People of Harrogate seem to be taking 'stay at home' message pretty seriously.'*

'The new politeness is keeping your distance from people,' said a fellow dog walker to me this week, as we proceeded to give each other a wide berth whilst out near the Showground. It's barely two and a half weeks ago since it felt slightly rude to suddenly veer off the footpath into the road in order to avoid someone whilst on the way to the local shop, now people are saying *'thank you'* when you do.

I had cause to make such a trip to our local shop last weekend for Paracetamol. I didn't particularly want to, but we were on the verge of running out and Molly had a migraine. On arrival, I spotted a man leaving the shop via the narrow access ramp and deliberately held well back in between two parked cars to allow him to leave at a safe distance.

Did I get a thank you or a nod of the head? Well, no. At this point, despite a myriad of different routes available to him to stay clear of me, he chose to squeeze past me between the two parked cars, head firmly down, seemingly oblivious to the fact we were in the middle of a pandemic and had to keep our distance. I just peered after him in disbelief, wanting to shout *'two metres!'* or something stronger, but realising there was absolutely no point.

Despite this, it has to be said that people in the small patch of Harrogate we're confined to, seem to be taking the *'stay at home'* and *'social distance when you need to go out'* messages pretty seriously, and that has to be a good thing. The hospitalisation of the prime minister* shows that this virus respects no one or anything.

So here we are into the third week of partial lockdown and moods have differed from day to day in this household, as they probably have in yours. One day you can be out in the garden with not a care in the world, and next day find yourself in a well of stress and worry as the latest news rolls in. I've found the key is to keep your brain active with positive things and not to dwell on possible scenarios that may or may not happen, difficult though that is.

Hence Molly and I have been getting to grips with FIFA on her new X-Box. Yes, I know we're a bit late to the party, but everyone has to start somewhere, and now seems the perfect time to do it. The only trouble is, we haven't mastered the art of shooting yet, so we ended up playing out three goalless draws in a row. In fairness, I haven't even mastered the art of picking out a pass, I just panic when I get the ball and 'hoof' it upfield aimlessly. So our matches consist mostly of Molly attacking and me putting in last ditch challenges and relying on a pretty good computer-controlled goalkeeper. That is until our fourth match in, when she lucked a 93rd minute winner.

Along with most of the country, we joined the 8pm clap for the NHS and other key workers last Thursday. It was a moment of touching poignancy, bringing a tear to my eyes at one point, as nearly everyone in the street emerged onto their front doorsteps to express their heartfelt thanks for everything these brave people are doing for us. Once we're the other side of this nightmare, things surely can't go back to business as usual; society has to change for the better and we need to ensure that these key people and services are respected, protected and properly funded.

*If you initially boast about shaking hands with infected patients in hospital, what can you expect? It must also be stated that Johnson commands not a single shred of respect in this household, either.

Getting nowhere fast. Random jottings from a third week of lockdown

Article originally published on Thursday 16th April 2020 under the title *'Town find themselves in complete state of uncertainty – but they're not alone.'* (Friday, Sunday and Monday didn't make the cut and appear here for the first time)

Thursday

I'm ruminating on how this would have been the bank holiday weekend where Town entertained Fylde before we all travelled to Stockport County on the Easter Monday, hopefully whilst in the thick of challenging for top spot. It's all a far cry from reality; who'd have thought a trip to Stockport would be so yearned for.

Today the National League is recommending that clubs vote to cancel the remaining normal season's matches up to 25th April, prior to issuing a set of options for concluding promotion and relegation issues. Every club in the National League will get an equal vote. We're told null and void is not going to be an option. It doesn't rule out play-off matches, and leaves Town in a state of complete uncertainty. But it isn't just Town.

For example, how do you decide final league positions when clubs have completed different numbers of matches?

Do you end with the table as it is now, or do you average out points per game? How can teams, especially those in the relegation zone, vote to end the season without knowing what the further options are? They could be voting for their eventual demotion.

Most importantly, the fact remains that we're still in the middle of a deadly pandemic where the UK may well turn out to be the worst-affected country in Europe, and we're not even at the top of the curve yet. We don't yet know how things are going to pan out, what the eventual exit strategy from lockdown will be, and whether the infection will return in any great numbers. According to the World Health Organisation, Covid-19 virus transmission declines at a far slower rate than it increases, and social distancing measures could well be with us for a very long time.

A phased return to some sort of normality, is not going to include restarting football matches with large crowds as one of the initial priorities, especially as sporting events and other social gatherings are the sort of places where clusters of the virus are thought to start up and spread. So would any subsequent play-off matches be played behind closed doors?

Of course, clubs could also vote against ending the normal season in the first instance.

It all leaves me even more confused than I was already. The National League appears more so, although admittedly under unprecedented circumstances.

Friday

My daughter and I are playing 'I Spy' whilst walking through the woods with the dog. There's not much to spot amongst the trees, so the game proceeds in quick fire fashion pretty much along the following lines.

'I spy, with my little eye, something beginning with t.'

'Tree.'

'No.'

'Trunk.'

'Got it... your turn.'

Fed up with Molly guessing everything first or second time, I struggle to decide between 'stone' and 'stick' for my go, eventually plumping for 'stone'.

'I spy, with my little eye, something beginning with s,' I say.

'Stone,' says Molly.

'No,' I lie, deciding to change mid-game to 'stick'.

There's a long pause and then one of the multitude of grey squirrels that the dog loves chasing pops into view.

'Squirrel!' shouts Molly. I'm feeling bad that I lied, as I normally play things straight, so I tell her she's got it. After all, she'll never know. Then she hits me with the following bombshell.

'Dad, I have a confession to make,' says Molly. *'When I was five or six, and we played I-Spy in the car, I used to pick two things beginning with the same letter and if you and mum guessed the first one, I'd change to the second one.'*

'Did you?' I reply, 'I'm shocked.' Butter certainly wouldn't melt in my mouth.

Worryingly, I fear we're spending so much time together under lockdown that she's beginning to read my mind.

Saturday

I'm walking through the woods again with the dog on my once-daily exercise allowance. I can hear the sound of a football being kicked hard in the distance, more so now the background noise of passing traffic on the main road has disappeared. I decide to veer off my normal route and skirt the grey metal fence past the St John Fisher School football pitches. In the first week following the suspension of the National League, I spent a fair amount of time watching grassroots matches on these pitches, whilst the dog sat bored in the background, hoping to be taken home. That's before even those matches were cancelled. So now here I am, standing in a clump of weeds, peering through the fence at someone I don't know smashing a football into a net in the far distance, in order to get my football fix. This is what it's come down to.

Sunday

After a long day pulling up weeds in the garden and washing up endless mountains of plates, dishes and cups generated by lockdown, I resolve to sand down and re-oil the kitchen worktop. I didn't think it particularly needed doing until we woke up last Friday morning to what looked like a crime scene. Some idiot, well ok me, had left a frozen bag of strawberries and blackberries out to thaw the night before, without putting them in a bowl. Cue a red blood-like substance oozing all over and into the wooden worktop and down the front of the drawers onto the floor. It takes me all evening to undo the damage. And to think I had such grand plans of reading lots of books I've never gotten round to starting and other such worthy things. I've so far managed half of 'Frankenstein' by Mary Shelley, something I determined to read last year after completing Bram Stoker's brilliant *'Dracula'*. Lockdown seems to be putting paid to me ever finishing it.

Monday

Today proceeded much the same as yesterday, except the oil was a second coat. My wife's been talking about the state of the wooden worktops for ages and how she'd like some new ones, whilst I buried my head in the sand. I may just have saved a lot of money.

Tuesday

Today I'm back at work in my small temporary home office. I made the mistake of asking everybody, whilst in a team meeting on Skype, if they'd been anywhere good over the weekend. I'm not sure the front room counts. Anyway, I've got to go, it's 11pm and the kitchen looks like a bomb site again. *'Frankenstein'* will just have to wait.

Repeat. If it's good enough for the BBC...

Article originally published in two parts on Thursday 23rd April and 30th April 2020 under the titles *'Looking back at Town's penultimate season in English football's sixth tier'* and *'Memories of Town's historic 2017/18 campaign – the season we went up!'*

Over the next couple of weeks, I'm going to take a slightly dewy-eyed trip down memory lane with a few recollections of Town's last two seasons in the National League North.

These reminisces were part of the very first unsolicited article I sent to the *Advertiser*, telling the story of how my daughter and I had lost our hearts to Town. They never saw the light of day as the article was so long that, even when edited down to half the size, it still occupied two pages of the newspaper. It was shortly after that I was approached to contribute a column, cataloguing Town's first season in the National League and the rest, as they say, is history.

I've retained the odd sentence from the original newspaper article to maintain continuity, and added to my original words as I think my writing's improved with age. Or, as my wife and the *Advertiser* editor will testify, *'Why use one word when three will do?'* I hope these snippets from the cutting room floor bring back a few memories.

My daughter's first ever away trip in the 2016/17 season was to The Shay, where she saw her favourite player, Jack Emmett, hammer in the only goal of the game from distance.

The other unfortunate standout memory from the day was watching Halifax fans boo fan hero Lloyd Kerry for perceived time-wasting, when he went down late on with a lengthy injury, prior to getting up and walking very slowly off the pitch. It transpired that Lloyd had sustained a fractured eye socket, a nasty injury that lead to him wearing a mask when he eventually made his comeback.

One of the highlights of that season, celebrated wildly by us, was Town hanging on to defeat Bradford Park Avenue by a solitary goal at Wetherby Road, despite only having nine men left on the pitch. To truly rub salt into Bradford's wounds, our keeper Peter Crook saved a penalty. And the rebound.

If the first sending off of Pittman just before half-time was justified, the second was a total injustice. Our goal machine at the time, Simon Ainge, was dismissed for a seemingly innocuous challenge in front of the corner flag, by a card-happy referee. Now, I work with someone who used to play for Bradford Park Avenue and was reliably informed that the offending Bradford defender felt a mere touch from Ainge, before collapsing like he'd been shot from behind, throwing in a melodramatic yelp for good effect.

Our emergency-centre-forward-in-an-injury-crisis Ainge banged, well mostly headed, in goal after goal that season, becoming the second highest scorer in the country behind Harry Kane. It was an even more impressive statistic when you realise he played the first four months of the season in central defence. There was one unforgettable spell when every Joe Leesley cross seemed to unerringly find Ainge's head like a guided missile.

My favourite chant of the season was reserved for the visit of Penistone Church in the Second Qualifying Round of the FA Cup. The Church brought around a hundred fans for their big day out and they elected to stand in the Kop next to the Town fans. During a quiet spell, the chant went up from the home fans, *'Shall we sing a song for you?'* On garnering no response, there was a long pause before one Town wag started up with *'All Things Bright and Beautiful...'* Church lost 3-0, but it was fantastic to see the enthusiasm and commitment of their supporters and players that day.

The season ended in anti-climax as Town slipped out of the play-off positions but it had still been a season of improvement off the pitch, with the average crowd nudging towards 1,000.

The following promotion season, Town raced into a 4-0 half-time lead at home to Alfreton, taking us back to the top of the league at the time. We then had to suffer the jitters as our opponents, Brendan Daniels and all, came a world class James Belshaw save away from squaring the match at 4-4.

A hapless FC United visited Wetherby Road and were duly dispatched by a score-line of 6-0.

Then there was York City. Twice.

An unsegregated 2,800 at Wetherby Road in September saw a 2-0 win for Town. It was all summed up perfectly by the Harrogate-based York fan on Facebook who revealed that he'd supported City all his life and had proudly taken his young son along to watch them for the first time. Now his son had repaid him by wanting to support Harrogate Town. Worse still, he was hankering after a Town shirt. Oh, how I felt for his dad. It must be hard, having to watch York City that is.

The return match at Bootham Crescent was even better. Town took an unprecedented 515 supporters, Jake Wright became a new short-lived folk hero, and Molly disappeared in a joyous ruck of fans rushing to the front of the terraces to celebrate the goals.

Of course, there were downs as well. In March, after defeating Gainsborough at home, the fake news came through that Kidderminster had hung on to defeat Salford 4-3, having been 4-0 up with ten minutes to go. We were back at the top on goal difference and the Kop celebrated with the manager and players. It was then that the tannoy crackled back into life: *'The news from Kidderminster is that Salford have pulled it back to 4-4.'* Our bubble was well and truly burst.

Town frustratingly suffered only their second home defeat of the season in the following game, 2-1 to a cynical time-wasting Spennymoor team, handing the advantage back to Salford in the process. I must, however, commend the victorious visiting players on taking the time at the end of the game to remind the Kop of just how many goals they'd scored via the considerate use of hand signals.

In the Play-Off Semi-Final, Town completely over-ran Chorley with slick, incisive passing movements and waves of attacks for the first half an hour, but the visitors' goal led a charmed life. When Chorley scored from their first effort on goal, heads dropped and nervousness set into the crowd. Cue the unusual sight of the Managing Director walking along the Wetherby Road Stand waving his arms and shouting at the crowd to turn the volume back up.

Then Town were awarded a penalty. Chorley fans ran forward and shook the net. It seemed to take an eternity for things to calm down and, when Knowles eventually despatched the spot kick, I couldn't believe it had gone in. I was just too tense to celebrate.

Ten man Chorley then basically shut up shop and we were heading into extra time when a speculative shot fell to Knowles in the fourth minute of injury time, for him to make it 2-1. I was sure he was offside. He had to be offside. I just stared at the linesman, awaiting the inevitable flag. It never came. The crowd went crazy like I'd never seen at Town before. In retrospect, I could have saved myself all that worry if I'd realised it was always meant to be. The Chorley manager had been cursed by the National League North Manager of the Month award prior to kick off.

A capacity 3,000 crammed into Wetherby Road for the Play-Off Final. Two more goals from Knowles and one from the National League North Player of the Season, Leesley, only told half the story. Town had two players stretchered off before half-time and, for all the talk of the visitors' mean defence, it was Town who defended like their lives depended on it when they had to.

It turned out to be Brackley who couldn't live with our pace and attacking desire, as evidenced by the third goal. As soon as Kerry nicked the ball in deep midfield, Ryan Fallowfield, our effervescent young full back raced down the right wing, hand aloft in the air. The ball to him was slightly over hit, but Ryan wasn't letting it go out, as he burst every sinew to reach it, before teeing up an incoming Leesley right in front of us at the Kop end.

We'd done it, we'd reached the top tier of non-league football: a whole tier above York City. It was two amazing firsts for little old Town.

'Maybe we'll be seeing no football at National League level until 2021 at the earliest'

Article originally published on Thursday 7th May 2020 under the title *'Promote the top two in each division and relegate no-one is my suggestion.'*

If you follow the news this week, talks are ongoing between the Premier League and Government with regards to finishing the Premier League season in June behind closed doors. We're told it would be a boost to the nation to see football back and, yes, it would, but surely not in this sense. Just consider, for a moment, the implications of bringing back just the Premier League.

Firstly, all playing staff and officials would need to be tested for Covid-19 on a regular basis, at great cost to the clubs concerned. This is at a time when valuable tests are lacking for key workers in general. If much needed tests were made available for footballers, would the public at large turn against this?

We have to remember that footballers are also family members. They all have homes to go back to, they may be living with vulnerable relatives, they may have underlying health conditions themselves. It would be their right to choose not to work in an environment that cannot possibly adhere to the 'new normal' of social distancing going forwards, and a number of Premier League doctors have expressed grave concerns over this today.

Considering the scenario where Premier League Football does restart, what happens the moment one member of staff tests positive for Covid-19? Surely under a necessary strategy of test, track, trace and isolate going forward, the entire club personnel will have to be put in isolation for fourteen days.

Then consider this is just the Premier League, a league awash with money. It becomes harder to envisage the Championship completing and, as for Leagues One and Two, playing on in front of empty stadia, even if possible, would push many clubs towards bankruptcy.

Where does that leave Harrogate Town? As much as I'd like to be positive about the way forward through this crisis, I'm afraid I find myself nodding firmly in agreement with the Boreham Wood Chairman this week, in that maybe we'll be seeing no football at National League level until 2021 at the earliest. Just let that statement sink in for a minute. Not only is this season finished, but business as usual next season may also not on the cards.

To my mind, the way forwards is clear. The Premier League, EFL and National League should stop looking after their own interests and work as one. They need to make a decision as to the conclusion of this season. And apply it consistently through the leagues. If it means making the season null and void, so be it. At least it treats all clubs the same.

My own approach would be to award the title to Liverpool and then promote the top two teams (based on points per game) consistently throughout the structure. It would mean a larger Premier League and National League for a short time, but it would be manageable. I would not relegate any team, just reward those who've done well.

With regards to next season, if it's going to start at all, it'll start late. So I'd look towards splitting the leagues into regional north and south divisions and run a shorter season. It should also just be played for pleasure, without promotion or relegation. That would remove some of the issues caused by any further outbreak of Covid-19 further down the line. Consider it our equivalent of the war-time leagues, so to speak.

I'd freeze this season's cup competitions and resume them next year, if possible. It's not as if squeezing new competitions into the calendar is going to be a good idea anytime soon, and completing cup competitions this year is not going to happen. What would be the point anyway, without fans?

Of course, all of this would benefit Harrogate Town, but I hope I'd say the same if we were in third position.

The other issue that may come to light going forward is that various clubs could find themselves going under. While I don't wish this on any club, the news that Town are currently rebuilding the Family Stand and bringing the ground capacity up to EFL required levels, is a piece of ambitious, forward thinking designed to give the message that Town are ready should they be required to step up.

That, for the record, is my twopence worth, but the truth is that we're still in the hands of an unseen virus that this country is nowhere near controlling at this point in time. Nobody has the answers yet as to a way forward.

Chapter Five
I get locked down but I get up again

National League play-offs and Wembley glory

It's going to happen!

Article originally published on Thursday 25th June 2020 under the title *'Town players must be sure to grasp promotion opportunity with both feet'*

It's been a strange three months or so for football, as with everything else.

With the season suspended for an unknown length of time, constant speculation has rumbled on as to when, and how, things would return. Of course, with the virus raging so strongly, no one could answer those questions with any authority, and I decided the best course of action would be to withdraw from football and all its speculation, treat it as a close season and, well, get on with other things as best I could in lockdown, whilst waiting for events to take their course. Football intruded only briefly when I managed to bump into Jack Emmett in Sainsbury's car park a few weeks ago.

So this week has been a bit of a milestone for two reasons.

Firstly, Premier League football returned, after a fashion.

As I'm too tight to pay for a Sky subscription, I tuned into Radio Five Live to listen to Manchester City versus Arsenal, but found myself switching off after ten minutes, dismayed at the lack of atmosphere and the commentators sounding almost as bored as I was. I didn't think anything could ever rival the tedium of listening to the Grand Prix on radio, and its two hours of angry buzzing bees with not a lot happening in between, but with no crowd noise to feed my imagination, this came close.

Undeterred, I found myself falling for the hype and sat down to watch the first live top flight match on the BBC since before the Premier League existed, well 1988 to be precise.

It's no little irony that I normally couldn't care less about Bournemouth versus Crystal Palace, and I'd bet that most of the other four million viewers couldn't either. Under normal circumstances this match would be last but one on Match of the Day and I would have missed it, having fallen asleep three matches in. But these aren't normal circumstances, and I was curious to view the spectacle of a match without fans.

Yet, try as I might, I just couldn't get into it and lost interest almost immediately, once Palace put two goals past a blatantly unfit and unprepared Bournemouth team. The second half was so lifeless that I fell asleep half way through. Some things never change.

I've since discovered that some of the Sky Premier League matches are also being shown on terrestrial TV, but I've decided there are more exciting things to do, such as mowing the lawn and vacuuming the carpets.

Growing up, as I did, listening to The Clash, I was dismayed when guitarist and one half of the song-writing duo, Mick Jones, was kicked out. This should have been the end of the band, but Joe Strummer and Paul Simonon staggered on, eventually splitting up after releasing an album called 'Cut The Crap' three years down the line. It was truly unlistenable, and the band really should have taken their own advice and called it a day three years earlier.

I use this analogy to sum up, for me, the return of the Premier League. It may also be an analogy for the return of my column this season, but I hope not.

I know it's good that things are slowly returning to a kind of normality but, with its empty stadia, canned crowd noise, post-lockdown hairdos and pre-season friendly vibe, the Premier League feels like a different competition, totally detached from the matches that were played up until lockdown. In my opinion, the season should have ended there and then, with everything decided on points per game and teams told to plan for next season. But then again, television money talks.

'Football is nothing without fans,' is the phrase that has often been trotted out in the past when supporters have been taken for granted by their clubs. I can now vouch for its accuracy.

The big news on the Town front this week was that the National League finally pulled their finger out and made a decision.

Barrow are to be crowned League Champions and promoted automatically, whilst Town will finish second and take part in the play-off semi-finals at the end of July for the second promotion spot. I was convinced play-offs would be impossible to undertake this summer, but it seems I may be proven wrong.

Approaching this from a 'glass half-empty' standpoint, Town can consider themselves unlucky. I genuinely thought we were beginning to close the gap on Barrow. It felt, after the 4-3 win at Chesterfield and Barrow's defeat to Notts County, as if we were serious championship contenders. We also had the small matter of the Cumbrians yet to visit Wetherby Road.

Approaching this from a 'glass half-full' standpoint, Town would have settled for second at the start of the season and a crack at the play-offs. There's also no guarantee that a rejuvenated Notts County wouldn't have caught us, and we still had to visit Meadow Lane.

We'll never know how the season would have panned out, of course, and everybody and everything has been affected by this crisis.

We are where we are, and Barrow are worthy, if somewhat 'fortunate', champions under the circumstances we find ourselves in. I say 'fortunate' because I'm pretty sure it's not the way they'd have liked to clinch promotion in an ideal world.

Although its four months since Town last kicked a ball, at least we're not having to pick up the league from where it left off, something which would have bankrupted clubs at our level, with no crowds and no big television money coming in to compensate.

The forthcoming play-offs should therefore be treated as a mini-competition in their own right, with Town but two victories away from Football League status. If we do gain that status, we'll have earned it.

My advice to the players, for what it's worth, as they head back into training this week would be to grasp this chance firmly with both feet. Take a lesson from our previous play-off victory and from rusty Bournemouth. Fitness and focus on the prize ahead will be key.

Nostalgia for an age yet to come

Article originally published on Thursday 2nd July 2020 under the title *'Making memories with my daughter that we will both remember for life.'*

To mark a hundred days since the announcement of lockdown, and to fill the void ahead of the looming play-offs, I thought I'd look back on some favourite moments from the season so far. Not wanting to repeat myself, having written in length throughout the season for this very newspaper, I decide to court a different opinion.

'Molly!' I shout up the stairs to my daughter.

'What?' comes the reply.

'Can you write down your favourite things from this season so far?' I ask.

Ten minutes later, this is what I get.

First on Molly's list is *'Beating Yeovil away.'* When questioned further, she says *'at the time it seemed so amazing, Yeovil were the best team in the league and it was my first massive trip, plus I high-fived Ryan Fallowfield at the end.'* Going back to the day in question, Town were just beginning to claw their way up the table, and Yeovil were on a run of eight wins in nine and would have gone top with a victory. I remember warning Molly that it may be a long way to go to watch a defeat. It was a very tough match and I was managing expectations. Saying that, there was never a doubt we were going. The coach was free, and I like a bargain.

Next up is *'Halifax away.'* I have to qualify this one, as we went there twice in quick succession, once in the League and once in the FA Cup. It turns out it's the cup match, and Molly's memory of it is the singing of *'Who put the ball in the Shaymen's net?'* as Mark Beck sunk the Shaymen for the second time in a matter of weeks. I trust she changed the rude word.

'Waiting for the Portsmouth game' is third on the list. Not the game itself, note, but the waiting for it in sweeping, cold rain for an hour outside the ground, as the floodlights failed. She remembers the holding up of illuminated mobile phones with her friends, as the lights failed again once inside the ground. *'But I thought you hated the cold and rain outside?'* I say. *'I'd like to go back there,'* she replies, *'I'd take any football nonsense at the moment.'* It's a fair point. So would I.

The fourth entry *is 'Fylde away and extra time'*. After the play-off disappointment there the previous season, this was payback time in the form of a chaotic, see-saw, extra-time, windswept Town victory in the FA Trophy. Molly remembers it as *'exciting, the wind kept blowing me away'* and for *'the chips in the pub'*. They were very good, I must admit. It's a shame we didn't have time for a second portion.

'Chesterfield before my b-day' is next on the list. *'I remember being on the coach at 11 'o' clock and it was nearly my birthday. We also won the football card,'* qualifies my daughter. Not to mention the fantastic 4-3 injury time victory by a Town team that was just magnificent, I also wish to interject. On the birthday front, Molly was the last of her friends to have a birthday party pre-lockdown: a great, noisy, music-filled night down at the local squash club.

The last item on the list is *'Chorley with their rundown ground'* and the comment that it was *'a big step down from Yeovil and Halifax'*. It therefore goes without saying that Victory Park is one of my favourite grounds to visit, albeit quite inappropriately named for the home team this season.

Realising that five of the six memories are away trips, Molly offers to think of some home memories, but I tell her that her first instincts are what I want. I must admit that it isn't the kind of list I was expecting. There are no great goals or on-the-pitch incidents, for example. She's helped, of course, by the fact that all the journeys were Town wins, and we gave Portsmouth an almighty scare in the FA Cup. And then I think about it a little more.

Many of my own favourite football memories from my earlier years in the Midlands mirror my daughter's memories, and are also triggered by off-the-pitch experiences and observations, together with memorable trips to different places. I clearly remember my first night match with my dad and the huge crowds outside the turnstiles, and I also have a vivid picture of a floodlight failure from when I was younger. I can recall the thrill of visiting new grounds, especially the mammoth trip to Torquay where I quit my job to go, and breathed a sigh of relief as an aquaplaning car narrowly missed us on the way into Devon. And I will never forget an early trip to a run-down Bolton ground with my dad as a thirteen year old where, in front of broken windows at the back of the stand, we watched our team score early and then withstand a major home team onslaught on a mud bath of a pitch, before exiting into tightly packed dark, northern, terraced streets. It was something I'd not really seen before.

When you're turning up at the same home ground week after week, it becomes familiar, enjoyable, exciting and comforting, but also partly routine. What you tend to remember is the time the visiting Wrexham fans shook the net or, indeed, the match when the floodlights failed. It's the way the memory works.

Reading Molly's list, I realise that I too have fond memories of those Town matches for the same reasons, apart from the birthday bit of course. But the main reason I'll remember those matches, is that I was experiencing them with my daughter for the first time, and I know that these memories will be with her for life also, just as my early football memories are with me.

One of the positives of lockdown has been the chance to spend a lot more time with my family, but I still hate this virus more than you could ever imagine, for taking away the prospect of coach trips with Molly to Notts County and Solihull, and the writing of more football memories.

Cardboard fans, a dilemma

Article originally published on Thursday 9th July 2020 under the title *'Do I want to be cut out in cardboard for Town's play-off semi-final clash?'*

As thoughts turn to the play-offs, Town fans are being invited to pay for photographs of themselves mounted on cardboard cut-outs to be placed in the ground, in order to witness the semi-final. It's a good, fun idea and I must admit to having given it some thought. Maybe, in hindsight, too much thought.

Firstly, and this is no small dilemma to start with, what expression would I choose for the photo? Most fans so far appear to be smiling, but what happens if, heaven forbid, Town go a goal down. A smile would be totally inappropriate in those circumstances. A downcast expression, on the other hand, says that I'm expecting us to lose, and that just wouldn't do, as we're meant to be visually cheering the place up. I think I'd probably just plump for a picture of myself biting my nails with a worried expression on my face, a standard posture I often adopt, and it fits all scenarios.

Next, there's the small problem of location, with my cut-out having to sit down. I'd like to ask to stand in the Wetherby Road stand or the Kop, but it wouldn't work without legs, and I don't do sitting down at a football match. Not if I can help it anyway. This week's *Advertiser* website declares that one or two 'lucky' cut-outs may even get to go into the changing rooms. That's a big no-no for me and, let's face it, the players would probably feel the same way, having me staring at them getting changed, whilst looking worried and biting my nails over in the corner.

Finally, and this really gets to the heart of the issue, I'm just too tight to fork out the required £20. I know I fork out that, and more, every time I go to an away match on the supporters' coach, but I've got a season ticket, so I'm reckoning my cut-out should be able to view the match for free!

When I ask Molly what she thinks about it she answers, *'Have you seen it's £20?'* So I'm pleased to see that we've bought her up to appreciate the value of money. When I then ask her where she'd like any cut-out of herself to appear, she replies, *'in the camera shed on the roof of the stand'*. Seeing as that's long disappeared to the tip, along with the rest of the old stand, I think we can safely rule that one out. I do have to say, though, that the pictures of the new stand rising up in its place this week look absolutely brilliant, even if I do regret missing the chance to ask for the camera shed to be dumped at my allotment, for old times' sake.

Whilst I couldn't possibly recommend placing a picture of Dominic Cummings in the seats, as witnessed at a recent Australian Rugby League encounter, even though he could plausibly have lost his way from Barnard Castle (his eyesight isn't what it was, I hear), I did think of maybe placing a picture of my dog there instead. That wouldn't be fair, however, as she actually isn't into football, choosing to run away at the slightest sight of a large football being kicked towards her. My wife also hates football, so that one's out too.

Maybe we could 'arrange for' Gareth Southgate to grace us with his presence, pretending that he's eyeing up the talent on display, ready for when England matches resume. But it again comes down to the issue of money.

I therefore have to say that, reluctantly, neither myself, or Molly, will be taking part in the cardboard cut-out scheme, but it goes without saying that I'm looking forward to seeing all those old faces I so miss in the stand.

And, if anyone wants to get their money's worth out of their cut-out after the match, I have an acquaintance who used to stand a life-size cut-out of himself in his front room to deter burglars when he was out, in the spirit of the cardboard police officer, lurking just inside the doorway of Poundland in town, looking out for shoplifters.

The shape of things to come

Article originally published on Thursday 16th July 2020 under the title 'What sort of an experience will match day be for football fans in the future?'

Having been in quite a flippant mood in last week's column, things are going to be heading off in a more thoughtful direction this week, as my mind turns to the way forward for the return of fans to football, and Town fans in particular, during this ongoing pandemic.

By this weekend, we will finally have some certainty as to our opponents in the Play-Off Semi Final. Otherwise, the only certainty is that everything else will remain uncertain as we move forward. I'm not only talking about events on the pitch here, because whatever league Town find themselves in next season, it will not be business as usual.

It's looking increasingly likely that capacity limits will be bought in, so that some form of social distancing can be maintained in grounds, whilst allowing teams to play in front of crowds. It's no different to the way that pubs, restaurants and live venues are being eased back in gradually. Town installing a new enlarged capacity in excess of 5,000 over the summer, now appears to be a moment of forward-thinking, especially if the capacity limit is to be based on a percentage of current capacity, even if we start the season in the National League North again.

One big question is whether away fans will be allowed to travel in these new circumstances. It's not only about providing accommodation in the grounds for visiting fans, of course. It's the whole issue around travelling to the game together in coaches, cars and on public transport, stopping at refreshment places and pubs on the way, thus potentially providing multiple vehicles of transmission for coronavirus clusters up and down the country.

So, where does this leave Harrogate Town Supporters Club and their away travel 'plans'? The short answer is that it's looking likely to be some time before coach travel to matches returns, in the same manner that indoor music events are currently some way off. Personally speaking, I wouldn't want to sit on a full coach with windows that don't open for several hours at this point in time, even with the compulsory introduction of masks; so this has to be a factor in any decision on away travel that I may choose to make. I presume there will be other people thinking the same way as me, as well as some who won't be.

Saying that, can you just imagine Town gaining promotion to the Football League for the first time in their history and then fans not being allowed to travel to games? Just imagine getting Bradford away first match in. I might just have to ask my work colleague if I can borrow his Bradford season ticket (for a price). But I'm getting hopelessly ahead of myself here.

It may also be that clubs are ordered to make home games all-ticket, with no admission allowed on the day, in order to stop away fans travelling, regulate numbers and areas, and to allow for quicker access to the ground without cash being involved. Can you just imagine the length of the socially distanced queues for the two sets of turnstiles along

Wetherby Road? Unfortunately, the club won't be able to stagger kick-off time! Presumably there will also have to be designated one-way routes laid out around the ground, and the 1919 will have to operate under strict guidelines, if it's allowed to open at all, whilst the match is ongoing.

With the plethora of scientific evidence out there indicating that shouting and singing spreads particles through the air much further, faster, thicker and wider than normal speech, is singing going to be frowned upon inside grounds? Are supporters going to be encouraged to wear masks to minimise infection spread in the short term and, indeed, to discourage singing and shouting? Are fans going to want to sing and shout so much anyway? How do you maintain social distancing in the Kop when Town score a last minute winner? Should designated spots be marked on the ground for people to stand on like outside our supermarkets? Will all spectators be required to hand over their contact details so they can be traced if they were standing in the vicinity of someone who comes down with the virus? All these are the sorts of questions the authorities will be struggling to come to terms with, in such a delicate situation.

Of course, all of this is entirely speculation, based on the assumption of coronavirus being around in the community at the current level for some time. How football will deal with any second spike in cases into the winter months will have to be factored in also. Might we see an enforced mid-winter break in this circumstance?

Whatever happens, we're going to have to get used to a new way of watching football for the foreseeable future, as we seek to return to some sort of normality, whilst looking out for others, by trying not to spread this awful disease.

Footnote: I wrote the bulk of this column before seeing a rumour on the internet that National League clubs will be allowed to fill one third of their stadiums next season, with the season start planned slightly earlier from mid-September onwards. Hopefully National League rules won't apply to Town, but anything along those lines has to be good news for football.

Waiting for the great leap forwards. Glasgow Celtic avoid friendly embarrassment as crunch time approaches

Article originally published on Thursday 23rd July 2020 under the title *'Whether Town go up or not, fans should remember that we've come a long way.'*

If it seems like an eternity since the final game of Town's coronavirus-truncated National League season, the few weeks following the announcement that the play-offs would be honoured have almost seemed to stand still. It's felt at times like we'd never get here but, exactly twenty weeks after Town's home draw with Bromley, the big weekend has finally arrived.

The decision not to play a warm-up friendly has been hotly debated amongst supporters online. Town don't have a big squad and need everyone to stay fit, so my own feelings on this is that basing at home and playing ten-a-side on the Wetherby Road pitch in front of empty stands is probably the best preparation the squad could get at this stage. Boreham Wood may come into this game with a couple of games under their belt, but Town have had the chance to replicate the match day situation, with everybody in the squad getting full ninety minute run-outs. I trust the manager on this, and I like the focused way in which Town seem to be approaching the play-offs.

Saying that, I was absolutely flabbergasted to read that Town turned down the chance to play a friendly match with Glasgow Celtic recently, and my heart sank for a very brief moment. Then I remembered that fans wouldn't have been able to attend anyway and I feel it would have been a distraction from Town's seemingly meticulous preparation. Maybe we can rearrange it for next year. I continue to live in hope.

As Covid-19 restrictions are still very much in place, it's hard to gauge the mood of the town as a whole, and there's no semblance of the usual momentum a team takes into the play-offs. It's simply a case of the players picking up from where they left off, and maintaining the confidence and focus they had in the weeks before lockdown.

With fans planning to watch on BT Sport either in the comfort of their own home, or in pre-booked, hopefully socially distanced pub settings, we're all with Simon and the players in spirit, even though we can't be there in person. Molly's booked a seat at her friend Lily's house. I've no idea where I'll be watching it yet, but I need to find somewhere quickly.

The club has received many good luck messages in the last couple of weeks and this, from Steven Capel, is the pick of them for me:

'My late father was a supporter of Harrogate Town when they were a Yorkshire League side. He would never have believed they would be anywhere near the Football League.

Come on lads do it for both yourselves, the town and his memory.'

If I was Simon Weaver, I'd enlarge it in bold text and stick it prominently on the dressing room wall. It's a beautiful message and sums the situation up perfectly. It also reminds us as Town fans, that whatever the outcome this weekend, let's not forget the massive strides forward this club has made, and is continuing to make, in its pursuit of the holy grail of League Football.

All that's left for me to say is good luck Town.

Action, time and vision. Coffee stains and a time lapse on the road to Wembley

Boreham Wood (H) (Play-Off Semi-Final) W 1-0. Goal: Muldoon. Crowd: 0. Article originally published on Thursday 30th July 2020 in the *Advertiser*'s 'Play-Off Final' pullout.

'Dad, I've knocked my coffee over,' says Molly.

'Go and get a towel to soak it up,' I reply, eyes glued firmly to the screen.

'But it'll smell if we don't clean it up now. And then we'll have to buy a new carpet,' she pleads.

'It can wait twenty minutes, and then we'll pull the settee out and clean it up properly,' I retort, after no more than a cursory glance in the spilt coffee's direction.

It's not the way I'd envisaged the celebrations, but Muldoon's just headed Town into the lead, and my daughter became rather over-excited in the process, throwing coffee everywhere. She'd not disappeared round to her friend's house to watch as originally planned, so we're both perched on the settee in the living room, heart rates off the scale.

I wasn't quite as surprised, as I'd seen the goal coming. Never had I been more certain that Town were going to score from the preceding corner. But before you begin to marvel at my clairvoyant ability, let me explain.

Just a couple of minutes earlier, my daughter's National League phone update had beeped. *'Dad, it says it's one nil to Harrogate,'* Molly had exclaimed. *'What? It must be a mistake. It's still nil-nil!'* I'd responded, incredulous but puzzled.

Then Town won the decisive corner and my brain slowly clicked into gear. Muldoon finding the net confirmed my suspicions. It wasn't a mistake, of course, we were watching on a two minute delay, and thankfully he didn't miss second time around. So much for 'live' TV. I tell my daughter to turn the mobile updates off.

Having been present at the Chorley match two years ago, I had thought that there was nothing more stressful than watching Town in a play-off semi-final. I was wrong. Watching Town in a play-off semi-final *on TV* is far more stressful. There's none of the usual match day routines, or people to talk to, in order to ease the nerves, and you feel that you can't influence the outcome. If I'd made it abundantly clear that watching football on television without crowds was pointless and dull, that was only because it wasn't my team on the screen at that particular time.

Pre-match, the new-Bolton manager, Ian Evatt, states that the visitors are the best side his now ex-Barrow team played all season, neatly forgetting that his Barrow players were affected by a virus the last time they met Boreham Wood and they still nicked a draw. He also neglects to factor in Town's 3-0 success at Holker Street, two matches into the season.

I needn't worry though. Watching the players march out on to the pitch, led by captain Falkingham in front of an empty stadium, with the new main stand occupied by cardboard cut-outs of people watching from home, it's obvious Town mean business. The look of steely determination is undeniable. There's no outward sign of nerves.

The commentators agree that Boreham Wood, having played a competitive game already, will have the slight advantage here, before Town proceed to run rings round their visitors for forty minutes, both in a footballing and fitness sense. It's breathtaking to watch. Any doubts have been dispelled; this team has both the energy and desire to match. There's a lovely bit, around twenty minutes in, where the camera zooms into Fallowfield, cracking a huge grin. His smile is matched only by the exuberance of his play. Simon Weaver has stated that this bunch of players is a pleasure to work with. I can confirm that they're a pleasure to watch too.

Our new signing, Aaron Martin, is looking keen and Jack Diamond's picked up where he left off. The only worry is that the first goal doesn't come, mostly due to a goalkeeper in form and a couple of good chances going begging. Boreham Wood then gain the upper hand in the period immediately before and after half-time, Belshaw turning one away with his leg and Hall blocking on the line. The game's now balanced on a knife-edge.

The only way Town are going to beat this goalkeeper is via something a bit different, hence Will Smith's header from the decisive corner, possibly heading towards Ashmore's safe hands, until Muldoon nicks in front of him to apply the faintest of touches. It's the first goal Town have scored against their visitors this season and we're in dreamland.

The commentators now wonder if Boreham Wood will be able to find any energy left in their legs, having already played a competitive match. You couldn't make stuff like this up. Except that they are, right here in front of us.

Stead comes close to making it two and, apart from a big head-in-hands scare when the visitors pull a shot wide, Town see the game out professionally, in front of the corner flag and into added time.

It's tense on the living room settee as four minutes of additional time are signalled. We're so close to a trip to Wembley. Well, the players are anyway. *'Turn your updates back on,'* I say to my anxious daughter in the ninety-second minute. That way we can hopefully save ourselves two minutes of unnecessary worry. The phone beeps. *'Full time!'* shrieks Molly, and we proceed to watch the final two minutes 'live' on TV whilst enjoying the first moments of relative calm that afternoon.

Now we can celebrate, knowing that the job's half done, there's a carpet still to clean and we have to go through all this again next week.

'We're a fit bunch of lads,' states a beaming Muldoon in the post-match interview. We never doubted it, and neither did the manager. Let's have the same again next week at Wembley please, Town.

These are the things that dreams are made of. Wembley glory brings the prospect of a trip to Bradford

Notts County (Play-Off Final) W 3-1. Goals: Thomson, Hall, Diamond. Crowd: 0. Article originally published on Thursday 6th August 2020 on the back page of the *Advertiser*'s 'Promotion Special' pullout.

It's Monday, the day after the greatest match in Town's history. Strolling with my family along the seafront at Newbiggin-On-Sea, our regular stop-off on the journey to Northumberland, I pause, as you do, to talk to a fellow dog owner. Having asked him if he lives in Newbiggin, he then enquires as to where we're from. *'Harrogate,'* I reply, half expecting a story about how he'd once been there and visited Betty's tea rooms. His face lights up in a smile of recognition and tells me that he'd been watching Harrogate Town on the television yesterday at Wembley. I point proudly to the Town badge on my jacket. He smiles again before adding, *'A load of my mates watched it too and said it was better than watching the Premier.'*

I'm now sat in a Northumberland hotel, twenty four hours after Town gained promotion to the Football League and, for the first time in eighty six columns, I had to take the dog for a long walk to compose my thoughts first, because I found myself completely and utterly lost for words.

Cast your mind back to the start of the season, if you will, it being an incredible 365 days from start to magical end. Callum Howe had just jumped ship for, as he saw it, the better bet in Solihull Moors (that worked out well). We witnessed the briefest of good starts, before suffering four defeats in a row. Couple this with discontent over ticket price rises, where five consecutive home matches saw attendances in the seven to nine hundreds, and all the good work of the season before seemed to be starting to unravel. It seemed as if the season in which we were hoping to witness this group of players push on from play-off quarter final defeat, was going to turn out to be a relegation scrap.

Of course this was all very early doors and the players maintained their belief, gradually dug in, turned round some positive results, culminating in a brilliant victory down in deepest Yeovil, before morphing into what many of us would consider to be the best team in the league. Anyone who's been watching Town over the past couple of seasons will know that this team of players were good enough to go all the way, as we started to push Barrow, but we scarcely dared dream, especially after the season was so cruelly cut short.

I mention all of this on the day after the greatest achievement in this club's history, simply because that stuttering start makes the team's achievement this season all the more incredible. I think we all need to learn never, ever to write this remarkable group of players off.

The conventional wisdom from the pundits before the Final yesterday was that, although the teams were closely matched, Notts County, with their history and tradition, were the favourites. We, of course, knew different.

Right from the kick off, Town took the game by the scruff of the neck in front of an eerily empty Wembley Stadium. Notts had known we were going to start fast and planned for it in the week before, but still they couldn't deal with it. Town just went out and played their own high pressing, passing game as if they were on the local park. Simon Weaver hinted as much in his pre-match interview; it was no secret, they know how we play, so let them worry about us. What quickly became apparent though, was that Town had also done their homework diligently, utilising more long balls than normal down the flanks, to ruthlessly expose County's defensive weaknesses. It's all well and good having a nice day out at Wembley, but it's all for nothing if you don't win, and Town had no intention of losing.

George Thomson epitomises the spirit of this team, having fought his way back into the reckoning after turning down a loan move earlier on in the season. At one stage he couldn't even make the first team squad, as he stood with the fans on the terraces at Fylde. Here, his energy and desire, driving into the area to make himself available for the quickest of crosses from a rampaging Fallowfield, paid dividends. One nil inside five minutes and we were daring to dream. Two nil at half-time was beyond our wildest dreams, but it really could and should have been four or five, as James Belshaw found himself the only spectator in the ground.

It wouldn't be Town, of course, without a scare, and County's goal, barely one minute into the second half, threatened to bring our dreams crashing down to earth. Surely Town weren't going to blow it now, we hoped. Notts came within a whisker of equalising. My daughter, covering her eyes, couldn't bear to watch. But this Town team is made of sterner stuff defensively these days and, crucially, has learnt how to see matches out that normally it would have lost or drawn. This was confirmed by my dad, a seasoned football watcher, who watched Town for the first time last week in the semi-final and, despite all their great attacking play, commented on the solidity of the defence.

It was the introduction of Jon Stead further up the pitch that helped turn the tide. A brilliant piece of footwork in midfield, an inch perfect pass to Muldoon out wide, who picked out the lone Diamond racing into the area in between two defenders to brilliantly cushion the ball home. It was a goal fit to grace the Premier League, and County heads visibly dropped. Stead even found time to bounce a shot off the post in added on time.

To see Town lift a trophy at Wembley and not be there in person was hard, but we have to take things as they come in this current situation. Immense credit must go to the Notts County players and management for the sporting way in which they conducted themselves after the game, staying around to applaud the victorious Town players, in the same way that Brackley did two years ago, even though they must have been hurting inside. I wish them well next season.

Times and teams like these don't come around very often in football. It could be said that this is Town's golden generation of players. It's a group that have largely grown up together from the National League North with a few honourable exceptions. The spine of Falkingham, Burrell and Kerry as good as anybody in the league. Yet, if I'm struggling to come to terms with the magnitude of the achievement of this entire squad, just think how 86 year old lifelong Town fan, Johnny Walker, is feeling this evening, having supported the club since the 1940s, when they had virtually no facilities to speak of and were called Harrogate Hotspurs.

And the beauty of all of this, is that this journey isn't finished yet. Town have the nucleus of a team that, on its day, is perfectly capable of going to Bolton, Grimsby, Walsall or Oldham and coming away with a result. Whether we'll get to see any of these games as travelling fans, is yet to be determined, as it won't be a normal season by any stretch of the imagination but, if you allow me to re-appropriate the words of an old National League North Town song... *'We're coming for you, we're coming for you, Bradford City, we're coming for you.'*

Family entertainment.
You wait for ages for a bus to come along and then two turn up in quick succession

Article originally published on Thursday 20th August 2020 under the title 'Fans breaching social distancing rules during historic bus parade? I think not.'

It's not often we get treated to an open-top victory bus parade in Harrogate, in fact it's never happened before in the history of the football club. Somehow, I don't think the winning of the West Riding County Challenge Cup, good though it must have been at the time, would have merited it.

Of course, when Town won the National League North title, we were able to celebrate with the players at the ground on the day. Covid-19 having put paid to all that at Wembley, today is the day that the fans finally get to celebrate in person with the players, albeit from a social distance.

As the bus is due to leave the ground and perform a non-stop circuit of the town before heading back again to the ground, I decide to have my fat rascal and eat it, by heading across the Stray, to cheer the players along West Park towards the Cenotaph, before heading back across the Stray in double quick time, to greet them again as they return to the ground. The dog will most certainly be pleased.

I ask Molly if she wants to come into town, but she says she's just going to go to the ground to watch with mum. Blimey, it must be a special occasion.

Actually, although my wife's never been to see Town play and isn't into football in the slightest, she figures the players have achieved something for the town that they should be applauded for, and she wants to go and see what all the fuss is about, seeing that her daughter and husband invest so much time and energy into watching the team.

Arriving breathlessly on to West Park in plenty of time, having crossed the Stray in a semi-excited speed walk, I tie the dog up to a fence behind me.

'Don't let me forget her,' I say to the person two metres away from me, only half-jokingly.

After what seems like an eternity, the players' bus comes round the Prince Of Wales Roundabout and onto West Park. Falkingham's up front brandishing the trophy as the bus passes, the street lined with cheering, socially distanced fans, curious shoppers, locals and the occasional bewildered dog. It's over in the blink of an eye, as the bus heads away from us towards the Cenotaph, the cheers growing louder as there's quite a crowd down there singing, *'Town are going up, going up, Town are going up.'*

I've no time to waste. Remembering to un-tether the dog, we head off in a jog back across the Stray. By the time we reach Wetherby Road, there's quite a crowd lining the footpaths. Molly's there with mum and two other friends from our street.

This time it's Ryan Fallowfield trying to climb on the front of the bus whilst hoisting the trophy aloft and, due to the traffic, the bus is travelling a little slower.

Under normal circumstances, the players would probably have disembarked at the ground, or at least stopped somewhere else, but stupid Covid's put paid to that too, so we watch the bus disappear into the distance down Wetherby Road towards the Showground.

It's been a brilliant hour or so, and a chance for fans, team and town to finally celebrate properly together.

Barely an hour later, the following report appears on the Daily Mail website:

'Harrogate Town supporters appeared to ignore social distancing rules as hundreds turned out for an open-top bus parade to celebrate the team's promotion to League Two. The North Yorkshire club reached the Football League for the first time in their 106-year history last weekend when they defeated Notts County 3-1 in the National League Promotion final at Wembley. Precautions such as the bus not stopping en route were put in place to try and avoid crowds during the Covid-19 pandemic but fans stood together anyway.'

It's a shame the pictures underneath the story contradict their version of events, and I can confirm that the people I saw cheering the victory parade were observing social distancing rules pretty much to the letter. We've been pretty good at that here in Harrogate.

It's then that I wonder whether all those other people on the beaches at Bournemouth and elsewhere were misrepresented in much the same way, by newspapers searching out a headline where none really exists.

Still, it's only a minor blemish on a day to remember. It would be nice to do this again next year though.